RESTORE. RECYCLE. REPURPOSE.

A
COUNTRY LIVING
BOOK

RESTORE. RECYCLE. REPURPOSE.

{ CREATE A BEAUTIFUL HOME }

Randy Florke WITH NANCY J. BECKER

HEARST BOOKS
A division of Sterling Publishing Co., Inc.

New York / London
www.sterlingpublishing.com

Library of Congress Cataloging-in-Publication Data:
Florke, Randy.
Restore. recycle. repurpose.: create a beautiful
home / Randy Florke with Nancy J. Becker.
p. cm.
"Country living."
ISBN 978-1-58816-769-9
1. Interior decoration—Environmental aspects. I. Becker, Nancy J. (Nancy Jane), 1956-
II. Title. III. Title: Eco-friendly guide to room-by-room decoration.
NK2113.F53 2010
747—dc22
                    2009026574

10 9 8 7 6

Published by Hearst Books
A division of Sterling Publishing Co., Inc.
387 Park Avenue South, New York, NY 10016

Country Living is a registered trademark of Hearst Communications, Inc.
www.countryliving.com

For information about custom editions, special sales, premium and corporate purchases, please contact Sterling Special Sales Department at 800-805-5489 or specialsales@sterlingpublishing.com.

Distributed in Canada by Sterling Publishing
c/o Canadian Manda Group, 165 Dufferin Street
Toronto, Ontario, Canada M6K 3H6

Distributed in Australia by Capricorn Link (Australia) Pty. Ltd.
P.O. Box 704, Windsor, NSW 2756 Australia

Design: Anna Christian

Manufactured in China

Sterling ISBN 978-1-58816-769-9

To my Grandma Alice.
Her frugal ways and generous heart
informs every page and all my days.

Contents

Introduction

As I sit down to write my second book about decorating your home or living space, spring is at full bore, which of course means that everything is coming up green. The trees are bursting with leaves, and flowers are blossoming everywhere; the miraculous season of growth is beginning once again.

The word "green" has taken on new meaning, representing not just color, but a new way of thinking and a new way of living. Articles, books, television programs, and an Oscar-winning film with former vice president Al Gore educate us about sustainable living, green products, and global warming. Information is always a good thing, but is sustainable living really a new idea? Where do you draw the line between buying "sustainable" products and sheer consumerism? How can we incorporate more eco-friendly ideas into everyday decorating?

I grew up on a hardscrabble farm in Iowa, where the biggest sin was waste and hand-me-downs were a way of life. We reused everything, from jars to fabric to the wood from demolished outbuildings. Glass jars became storage containers in the larder, and the plaid flannel from a favorite shirt lived on in the patches of a crazy quilt on my bed. Nowadays they call that repurposing; then we called it another day on the farm.

The idea of sustainability also predates my immediate ancestors. The lives of North America's indigenous people were inextricably bound to the land around them. They gathered what they needed to survive from the local forests and fields, and they used almost all of what they harvested, with very little waste. The Inuits relied on the right whale for everything from food to fuel to housing materials, taking only a few whales a year and hunting from kayaks using stone harpoons. Even New England whalers in the late seventeenth century used most of the right whale carcass, producing oil from

OPPOSITE PAGE: An old tin floral bucket is the perfect home for locally grown flowers, and one of the first objects I repurposed for decoration.

blubber and using every bit of whale bone in products like corset ribbing, umbrella frames, chair caning, and many products now made of plastic. As New England whalers developed more powerful technology, however, the whale population decreased, and whalers moved beyond the American coast to more remote waters rather than keeping their activities at a sustainable level. Modern whaling practices have continued this trend and taken a toll on all manner of sea life.

While most of us would be reluctant to fully emulate the Amish, Mennonites, or Shakers—many of whom live today without conveniences like electricity, telephones, and cars—we can take pages from their stories. Appreciating the value of simple, pared-down clothing and interiors furnished with durable items that become family heirlooms can inform our buying habits and our way of thinking.

Any wealthy traveler visiting an impoverished area can't help but notice that containers and clothing, building materials and old equipment are reused and repurposed, with large aluminum cans converted into water carriers or dust pans, and sheets of corrugated metal continuing on as a roof or a wall. Many people throughout the world live this way because they simply have no choice, and their reuse of material is the result of abject poverty, which should never be glamorized. Acknowledging this kind of reuse—reuse born of necessity— takes us one step closer to the realization that all our planet's resources are limited. We have a responsibility to safeguard those resources, and we must take it seriously.

Perhaps this is a romanticized view of history, but I like to think that our ancestors' everyday actions were guided by an innate sense of frugality, efficiency, and conservation. We can be inspired as much by that spirit as by the confines of a limited budget when we go about renovating or decorating a room.

BUYING INTO GREEN?

Watch nearly any of the decorating or renovating shows aired these days and you'll see fine examples of rooms recast into models of respectable sustain-ability. Recycled glass tile, bamboo floors, organic fabrics, radiant heating systems, salvaged marble countertops, and locally crafted furniture are all very eco-friendly, and no doubt the rooms themselves are gorgeous—but at what price? These designs often reflect not only huge expense but a great deal of consumerism. What became of the pre-renovation cabinets, the linoleum flooring, and the ceramic tile? Have they ended up in the local landfill?

ABOVE: Although these cabinets weren't made by Shakers, they have a stark simplicity that I love, as well as the sensible utility of a traditional piece.
OPPOSITE PAGE: Nothing is more eco-friendly than refreshing an outdoor shed as a guesthouse.

Rather than buy new bricks, I used recycled, which adds both vintage and environmental cachet.

Our very notion of "home" has been supersized; everyone seems to covet a "great" room and a master suite, a six-burner chef's stove and a two-car garage. Perfectly good houses are razed so McMansions can rise on that same half-acre lot. Are we losing our ability to live simply and responsibly?

Questions like these are why I think sustainable living truly begins at home. It's where we eat, sleep, dream, and dress; it's where we cook, clean, nurture, and nest. Home is where it all comes full circle. This book explains how we can decorate our homes without spending barrels of money, without doing a lot of consuming, without shipping in costly materials from far-flung places, and without adding to the piles of refuse at the nearest dump.

ABOVE: This pretty house in the country needed a lot of TLC when I found it, along with a new chimney.
OPPOSITE PAGE: The walls are not just green hued but finished with low-VOC paints; the fireplace mantel and decorative objects are vintage, and the flora are locally grown. A side chair upholstered in organic fabrics completes the picture.

This stainless steel table topped with a hard-working butcher block takes the place of an island. Note the wonderful restaurant-inspired Wolf stove! Try picking one of these up at a restaurant close-out sale.

Decorating, and the way you go about it, can have a serious impact on the environment, both within the home and outside of it. My hope is for the pages of this book to provide you with a full range of ideas for "going green" in both décor and lifestyle. You shouldn't have to sacrifice aesthetics to decorate in an eco-friendly way, nor should living frugally mean that your rooms resemble the quarters of a Buddhist monk. From exploring new ways of reusing old items to paring down for a simpler life, and from refurbishing in eco-friendly ways to buying green when you must purchase new, I hope to tempt you with ideas and interiors that please the eye, are easy on the pocketbook, and care for the planet.

Room by room, I present ideas, examples, and resources in shades of green. Since I employ a layer-by-layer approach to decorating all my rooms, I bring that sensibility to this book, with a major focus—or layer—for each room: flooring in entryways, countertops and cabinets in the kitchen. We'll settle into upholstered furniture in the living room, and in the bedroom, we'll consider the major comfort factors of beds, bedding, and paint and wall coverings. The focus in the bathroom is vanities, sinks, and tubs. Chapter 5 explores the home office, from desks to storage—to carving out a space for both. Then we'll step outside and do some outdoor living and entertaining. Regardless of the room or the design challenge, the focus will be on using sustainable materials and repurposing existing items.

The rich vein of wisdom from those who came before will be explored in side-bars called Grandmother's Tips. I'll plumb the full depths of my flea market and thrift shopping skills, since to me, antiquing is the ultimate in living sustainably. Wherever possible, we'll explore how to get the whole family involved in a more eco-friendly lifestyle. Without getting too Green 101 on you, I'll explain a few terms straightaway. What would life be without a few indulgences? I'll show you how a sacrifice in one area will let you glam it up in another.

At this point in history, we are all focused—and rightly so—on the environment and the many ways that we can reduce the human impact on both our immediate surroundings and the planet. But what I really hope you'll take away from these pages is how much fun it is to create a room on a modest budget and with an eye toward reuse and sustainability. The process of finding the right objects and materials, taking an active role in transforming the pieces that you live with, and thinking about how all these parts come together in welcoming, lovely, and earth-friendly décor should not be a duty or a chore that begins and ends, but rather a joyful and ongoing part of life.

ABOVE: An old rubber inner tube: a classic swing for the tree or a makeshift champagne bucket? You decide.
OPPOSITE PAGE: Vintage signs and dollhouses make the perfect accessories for a young girl's home.

Defining Green
TERMS USED THROUGHOUT THE BOOK

AERATOR: A small, inexpensive cap that fits on a faucet to reduce water consumption.

CARBON FOOTPRINT: A measurement of an individual or corporation's contribution to carbon dioxide (CO_2) emissions. Like other "greenhouse gases," the CO_2 in the earth's atmosphere is essential for the warmth of our planet but can raise the temperature to lethal levels in excessive amounts. Cars, airplanes, burning coal, and clear-cutting forests all raise the levels of CO_2 in the atmosphere. Approximately 40 percent of an average American's contribution to CO_2 emissions comes from the use of appliances such as stoves, refrigerators, microwave ovens, televisions, air conditioners, lights, and computers. The ultimate goal of measuring one's carbon footprint is to reduce it as much as possible.

CARBON NEUTRAL: A process that balances the amount of CO_2 released with the amount offset by the creation of more eco-friendly energy sources. For example, a frequent driver might plant trees that absorb the amount of CO_2 emitted by his car.

COMPACT FLUORESCENT LIGHTBULB (CFL): A bulb that uses fluorescent elements rather than heat-wasting incandescent elements. CFLs last much longer than incandescents and use less energy. They do contain a small amount of mercury and must therefore be disposed of properly.

ENERGY STAR APPLIANCES: Products that consume less energy and therefore reduce emissions of greenhouse gases, labeled "Energy Star" appliances through a voluntary labeling program of the U.S. Department of Energy (DOE) and the U.S. Environmental Protection Agency (EPA). Consumers can save money and protect the environment by purchasing products with the Energy Star label.

OPPOSITE PAGE: Talk about low emissions! A Victrola has no carbon footprint because it runs on muscle. Just don't expect to find Jay-Z on those old 78s.

FOREST STEWARDSHIP COUNCIL (FSC): A nonprofit, nongovernmental organization that promotes responsible management of the world's forests by establishing standards for harvesting forest resources. Consumers can use FSC company ratings to purchase goods only from those organizations that harvest responsibly. Landowners and companies that sell timber seeking FSC certification must meet principles that provide environmental protection, conserve ecosystems, respect indigenous peoples' and workers' rights, comply with local laws, and manage the scale of the operation, among other things. Independent certifiers using these principles and criteria assess forest management for the FSC. Manufacturers of wood products can also get FSC certification through a slightly different process that tracks a material's chain of custody.

GREEN: A general term for a product or process that produces less waste, and uses fewer natural resources and less energy, than its conventional equivalent. Green concepts can be incorporated into everyday life as we consider how objects are consumed and disposed of.

GREENHOUSE GASES (GHGs): Gases like carbon dioxide that warm the earth's atmosphere and make it habitable. GHGs are produced by both natural and industrial processes. In excess quantities, GHGs could raise the global temperatures to levels that would render the earth uninhabitable.

GRAY WATER: Residential wastewater from dishwashing, laundry, and bathing that can be recycled for irrigation if properly treated.

LEADERSHIP IN ENERGY AND ENVIRONMENTAL DESIGN (LEED): A rating system developed by the U.S. Green Building Council to provide standards for eco-friendly construction.

NATIVE PLANTS: Plants that occur naturally in a region or environment and thrive without fertilizers, pesticides, or excessive amounts of water.

OFF-GASSING: The process by which new materials such as paint, adhesives, textiles, and building materials emit potentially hazardous gases into the atmosphere.

ORGANIC: A term applied to foods and other agricultural products that are grown, processed, manufactured, and shipped without the use of pesticides, fertilizers, or other harmful chemicals. Various nations and regions have established different criteria that a product must meet in order to be certified organic.

SUSTAINABLE: Produced and used in a way that balances consumption with regrowth and can be continued indefinitely. For example, bamboo is considered a sustainable wood because it grows quickly and is therefore easily replenished, but harvesting practices must also be sustainable or even bamboo forests will vanish.

VOLATILE ORGANIC COMPOUNDS (VOCs): Solvent additives—found in higher levels in oil-based paints and to a lesser degree in water-based latex paints—that emit potentially harmful gases. Many companies have begun producing low- or no-VOC paints and lacquers, but according to an article by Sarah Kershaw in *The New York Times*, low-VOC paints can be more expensive and produce mixed results, requiring more applications—and therefore more waste—than ordinary latex paints.

WASTE STREAM: The waste continually produced by and discarded from homes and businesses. Everything from trash to dirty water is included in this concept.

Entryways

WELCOME TO MY WORLD

The restored wooden foors of this hard-working entryway are protected from overuse with a rag rug runner. **ABOVE:** Two takes on green. Vintage American pottery is green by virtue of both its age and its hue.

I HAVE OFTEN WONDERED WHAT IT WOULD BE LIKE TO BE a door-to-door salesman—not because I'm particularly good at selling things, but because of the chance it would afford me to peek into so many different homes. Entryways have always fascinated me, from rent-controlled New York City apartments lined with thousands of LPs to country house mudrooms complete with wooden pegs for overcoats and a sturdy bench for donning shoes.

Entryways can be a microcosm of personality. They are small, transitional spaces where people generally don't linger, so you can play out colors, textures,

Did You Know?

According to the U.S. Environmental Protection Agency (EPA), if every American household simply replaced one incandescent bulb with a compact fluorescent light bulb (CFL), it would do as much to lower the country's annual greenhouse gas emissions as taking 800,000 cars off the road.

RIGHT: A double screen door leading out to the porch makes a grand yet welcoming entry for guests

OPPOSITE PAGE: Although I personally picked out each and every rock that I used in this entryway, there are many sources closer at hand and more user-friendly. The end result of using these "found" organic materials is simply beautiful.

RESTORE. RECYCLE. REPURPOSE.

*Reclaimed wood floors can make
a new home seem aged and beautiful.*

and other decorating ideas that might be overwhelming in a larger space. Patterned wallpaper, saturated paint colors, unique flooring, a large piece of art, or a small collection of interesting objects can have a stunning effect.

People who are about to make decorating decisions often are paralyzed by the many possibilities. When the sheer number of choices makes the task daunting, turn to the principles of environmentally conscious design to make the whole process simpler and more streamlined. Why not use the idea of greening the entryway, or any room, as a way to settle some of the difficult design decisions? Commit to purchasing only second-hand items, reducing waste and saving yourself from having to choose from among countless new objects.

Paint: Use only VOC-free paints, which don't give off harmful gasses. (You can get VOC-free paints at big-box stores like Home Depot or any specialty paint store.)

Wallpaper: Since entryways are small, you can probably find vintage wallpaper in sufficient quantity. Check out Secondhand Rose (http://www.secondhandrose.com/) or eBay (http://www.ebay.com/) for vintage finds.

Furnishings: Use antique or collectible furniture in the entryway.

Art: Purchase paintings at a flea market, buy vintage photographs, or make your own.

FOCUS: FLOORING

For the entryway chapter, we're going to focus our attention downward. The number of sustainable flooring options has increased tremendously in the last few years. Entryways are small enough that your design dollars will go far, though all the materials that we will consider here can work in virtually any room. Before I tear up any old flooring, though, I try to make the best of what's already there. If a hardwood floor can be refinished, stained, or even painted, that's far preferable to tearing it up and adding refuse to the nearest landfill. If the floor simply must go, I look for sustainable materials that pack the most green for the buck.

Reclaimed Wood

Use aged pine from an old farmhouse, seasoned oak from a razed barn, or wormy maple from a rural outbuilding. Wood from demolished structures is often reclaimed rather than burned and can be incorporated in new projects with beautiful results. Repurposed wood doesn't come cheap, but the patina from ancient lumber is as rich and earthy as the taste of aged wine. One source

ABOVE: Because stone is of the earth, it's naturally beautiful. Choose slate and sandstone, which come from the least invasive mines.
OPPOSITE PAGE: Beautiful old wood floors like these deserve to outlive us all, and under the right caretakers, they will.

to check out is Terramai (http://www.terramai.com/); it offers reclaimed woods that are Forest Stewardship Council (FSC) certified.

Bamboo

Bamboo is considered environmentally friendly because it grows quickly with little fertilization. Purchase it from a manufacturer that can certify that fair trade practices were used to obtain it. Bamboo isn't as durable as hardwoods such as maple, and when maple is derived locally from carefully harvested forests, it may be just as good an option. Remember that bamboo is typically grown in far-flung places and that shipping materials long distances uses fuel and creates pollution, mitigating their eco-friendly qualities.

Stone

Few materials are as naturally beautiful as stone flooring, and entryways are an ideal location for it, since stone is both durable and water resistant. Stone is not a renewable resource, however: it takes millions of years to degrade, and the very act of excavation is damaging to the environment. That being said,

RIGHT: Not only is stone beautiful, but it's easy to clean and maintain—the perfect combination for an entryway.
OPPOSITE PAGE: Brick has been recycled from time immemorial. Here it is both beautiful and tough in a mudroom entryway.

there are levels of green when it comes to choosing stone. Slate and sandstone are the more eco-friendly materials, since they require less intrusive forms of mining than materials like marble or granite that lie deep within the earth. Before purchasing stone, find out how it was excavated and consider one that has the least invasive process. As with wood, shipping stone far distances increases the product's carbon footprint, so try to find a local source.

ABOVE: Look for vintage doorknobs at flea markets and salvage shops; they're the perfect jewelry for a vintage door.
RIGHT: Another view of the rock flooring in an entryway, along with an old bench I picked up at a flea market. The bench makes a handy place for kids to remove muddy boots.

Cork

Cork is a more renewable resource than many woods because the trees are not destroyed when the cork is harvested. Its insulating, antimicrobial, and sound-proofing qualities are also touted by manufacturers. And it comes in a variety of hues, not just the color you get from a wine bottle!

Paint

If your entryway floors are wood and have seen better days, consider painting them. I'm not talking about painting gorgeous old floors that have earned a warm luster, but floors that are too worn and scuffed to be properly refinished. How about black and white checkerboard or a faux carpet design á la trompe l'oeil? Or go with pure black or white—the glossier the better. The impact on the earth is minimal, especially if you use VOC-free paints.

WALLFLOWERS AND OTHER WALL COVERINGS

The small bit of wall in the average entryway represents a great place to conduct a design experiment. Try out bold color, wallpaper, or collages created with found materials. From vintage wallpapers, which are usually only available in small quantities, to alternative coverings, like gift wrap or specialty paper, you can let your imagination go wild in an entryway. Photocopy old books, Chinese calligraphy, or architectural drawings and paper the walls with them. Use a sponge and white craft glue diluted with water to smooth on delicate papers, experimenting first for durability. If you absolutely have to buy new, look for chlorine-free, recycled paper or vegetable-dyed jute coverings.

FURNISHING

The furniture in my entryways always started life as something else: a church pew or school bench now used for removing shoes; a plaster bust, now the perfect resting place for a hat. I wouldn't think of purchasing a brand new umbrella stand when there are all sorts of interesting pots, wooden barrels, and ceramic planters that can do double duty. Existing objects are far more interesting than anything you could buy new.

Rocks have little impact on the environment compared to the mining of other flooring materials.

Paint the Floor Red! Handy Tips for Floor Painting

☞ Wear a mask while sanding and painting.

☞ Mask off baseboards with painter's tape for a masterful job.

☞ Sand first; use an electric sander, or even do it by hand.

☞ Make sure the surface is free of dirt and debris before painting.

☞ Use floor, deck, or porch paint. Get the color of your choice mixed at any big-box store.

☞ Use VOC-free paints and finishes.

☞ Always prime before painting; this is especially critical for a floor.

☞ Put down two or three coats of paint and a finishing coat of polyurethane or varnish.

☞ Let each coat dry at least twenty-four hours before laying down another.

ABOVE: Do away with plastic shopping bags entirely. Instead, keep reusable cloth bags in the entryway to take along with you on your next shopping trip. Any reusable bag will do, but why not take the opportunity to preach a little green?
RIGHT: The large mirror in the entryway of my apartment may have seen better days, but I like her just the way she is: a woman of a certain age who's got style! Entryways are also the perfect place for an umbrella stand.

Third Place
Green

Who doesn't like flowers in the entryway? But flowers often travel on airplanes from far-flung places, which puts huge amounts of carbon dioxide into the atmosphere. Use locally grown produce to decorate the entryway: pumpkins or squash, potted plants, garden flowers, or herbs. Growing plants absorb CO_2 instead of emitting it.

Second Place
Silver

Pump up the volume of your sustainable buying habits and get out of the plastic bag habit. Millions of plastic bags end up in the waste stream outside of landfills, getting caught on trees and blocking the drains in streets and sewer systems. Even in landfills, plastic bags take anywhere from months to hundreds of years to decompose.

First Place
Gold

Eschew paint altogether! That way you'll never have to worry about paint fumes and dealing with old paint cans. I recycled this old framed mirror for our front entryway in New York City and decided not to paint it at all. I liked its slightly worn sensibility—like a genteel, but faded, grande dame.

Try to think out of the box when it comes to entryway furniture. Take that bowed, glass-front cabinet you inherited from an aunt, paint the trim white (or orange), and use it for your collection of pottery. Top a brightly painted nightstand with a tall lamp; it's the perfect catch-all for keys and gloves, and you can stash menus or shopping bags in the top drawer. Even bookcases can take pride of place in an entryway: imagine a few shelves of travel books or a growing collection of Modern Library classics with their multicolored book jackets. Used books covering a particular subject are another fun thing to collect.

DOORS

Don't forget about the portal to your world! Doors come in a huge variety of styles, colors, and sizes, and vintage options abound. If you opt for something modern, look for Energy Star-rated doors with a low U-value, which represents how long it takes for heat to transfer through the door and its frame. This will help keep your house snugly insulated.

Installing a vintage front door is best left to professionals since size, fit, and weatherproofing are all critical. If the existing door is vintage and you want to make it more weatherproof, consider installing a storm door.

ACCESSORIES

Mirror, mirror, on the wall. What better place than the entryway for a mirror, and what better mirror than one with patina and age? Loads of great mirrors are available at every flea market, garage sale, and thrift shop. Etched or beveled, slightly de-silvered or sporting chipped frames, older mirrors have style. If one mirror is chic, then try hanging three circular mirrors, or make a wall of mirrors with frames of varying shapes. You can never have too many, especially in a place where you need to take one last look before taking on the world.

Entryways are also the place to experiment with accessories that might seem odd or overbearing somewhere else. A friend of mine features a collection of taxidermy—vintage, of course—in her entryway. Another has a collection of colorful 1960s glass. I like clocks in the entryway, too. Vintage clocks are great fun to collect. Look for those with wind-up mechanisms, and do away with the need for batteries, which require special disposal. When simply tossed in the trash, they get sent to a landfill, and the heavy metal in the batteries leaches slowly into the soil, contaminating the groundwater or surface water.

OPPOSITE PAGE, CLOCKWISE FROM LEFT: Classic wooden door with transom, so good-looking you might not notice it. ❄ I covered my CFLs with small black shades. The vintage ceiling medallion and shades are the perfect masquerade for the newfangled and some-what unsightly but energy-efficient bulbs. ❄ Vintage glass doorknobs are a great accessory, whether replacing the actual hardware on a door or displayed as a collection in a bowl. ❄ Decorating with local produce makes a lot of sense economically and environmentally, since exotic flowers are often flown in from equally exotic locales. After it decorates your entryway for a little while, use the pumpkin or squash in soups and casseroles.

Nothing says "welcome home" better than a sturdy bench for slipping off shoes.

Ultimately, an entryway is a place where you can be a little experimental, since it is a space of transition rather than rest. Don't be surprised when your guests collect in the entryway during parties and social events, though, especially when you provide them with some great focal points.

LIGHT MY WAY

If an entryway is the first glimpse of the homeowner's personality, then lighting can establish mood. Effervescent or romantic? Playful or subdued? Entryways need good lighting, and since lamps and fixtures are integral to a design scheme and fun to scout out and buy, they're always prominently featured in my décor.

In the entryway I often marry older fixtures with compact fluorescent lightbulbs. Light fixtures are generally simply designed, and as long as you get a qualified electrician to check them out and help install them, vintage fixtures are safe, affordable, and green. You can add CFL bulbs, which are now available in many shapes and configurations, to almost any fixture. Don't like the look of CFLs? Cover them with mini shades. Don't forget the possibility of a table lamp or even a standing lamp in the entryway. Yard sales or collectible shops often feature single lamps of milk glass or alabaster from the 1940s and '50s that have survived without their mates. They're great for topping a small piece of furniture and offer a cheerful welcome in the entryway. Even if you have an overhead fixture, additional lamps can help you create a particular mood.

OPPOSITE PAGE: Stairway to pumpkin heaven!

Choosing a Compact Fluorescent Lightbulb

According to the Energy Star Web site, CFL bulbs use 75 percent less energy than incandescent bulbs and can last ten times longer. It's important to choose the right CFL for the job.

☞ Spiral CFLs are the most common and can be used wherever traditional bulbs were used.

☞ A-shaped CFLs look similar to traditional bulbs but have the same energy-saving characteristics as spiral CFLs.

☞ Globe CFLs are meant to be seen and should be used in bathroom vanities or on the ceiling if they will be visible.

☞ Tube bulbs work just like the spiral bulbs but are streamlined to fit into wall sconces.

☞ Candle-shaped CFLs are perfect for sconces or fixtures in which the bulb is visible and a decorative flame style is desired.

☞ CFLs are also available in indoor and outdoor reflector, three-way- and dimmer models.

Kitchens
COOKIN' IT OLD SCHOOL

Can you count all the recycled items used in this country kitchen? Check out the vintage wallpaper decorating the walls, the salvaged baskets and pottery, and the beadboard, which looks lovely restored on the walls. **ABOVE:** These PaperStone countertops are made from 100 percent recycled paper. The bowl is vintage spongeware.

IF A HOME IS A METAPHOR FOR THE HUMAN BODY, THEN the kitchen is truly the heart, the place from which so many good things emanate. On cold winter mornings on the farm in Iowa, once I finally got myself out of bed, I hurried to the kitchen, where the warmth from the stove and the aroma of a hot breakfast were like a welcoming embrace. Even though I didn't cook, one of the first things I bought at a yard sale was a slotted spoon made of stainless steel and wood. I have no idea why I bought it: the nickel it cost me? Its perfect balance in the hand? The sheer utility of it? I still have that spoon thirty years later, and I can honestly say it's one of my favorite utensils, the one I reach for again and again.

That's the way a kitchen should be: replete with good materials that are up to the job at hand and simple, ergonomic design that transcends the trends. Not only are some of the home's big-ticket items and major energy guzzlers—like refrigerators, stoves and ovens, and dishwashers—found in the kitchen, but flooring, cabinetry, countertops, backsplashes, and other fixtures can quickly become dated. When casting about for rooms to redo, most folks immediately focus on their kitchens, which represent many ways to reduce, reuse, and recycle.

The repeat of the grid pattern in the window panes, tiles, and wooden cabinets gives the whole thing a modern-meets-country look.

OPPOSITE PAGE: Square ceramic tiles cover both the backsplash and the counters in this country kitchen, and I applaud the homeowner for preserving them rather than tearing them out.

Cost is frequently a major consideration when doing any sort of renovation work. Sure, with an unlimited budget, anyone can redo a kitchen with the latest appliances, sustainable materials, brand new surfaces, and cabinetry, but who has an unlimited budget? Replacing everything in the kitchen also means that the old appliances, cabinets, and flooring have to go somewhere—usually

the nearest landfill. The key is finding a good middle ground: repurposing existing surfaces and fixtures whenever possible to reduce both costs and waste, and when items must be replaced, searching for the most cost- and energy-efficient way to do so.

Let's look at sustainable ways to a beautiful kitchen. Since countertops and cabinets play a starring role in the kitchen and are among the first things homeowners want to change, they're the focus of this chapter.

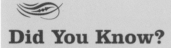

Did You Know?

Natural stones like marble and granite can be stained or damaged easily by busy chefs and active families, so greener solutions are often practical solutions.

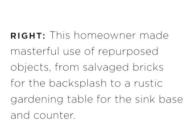

RIGHT: This homeowner made masterful use of repurposed objects, from salvaged bricks for the backsplash to a rustic gardening table for the sink base and counter.

OPPOSITE PAGE: Here a rustic table fills in beautifully for the kitchen island.

Note the use of a mirror as an alternative to a backsplash.

COUNTERTOPS

Ask any home chef the essential ingredient to a recipe and before she says "virgin olive oil" or "fresh herbs," you'll hear "counter space." Every cook wants counters made from materials that can fend off the sharpest knives and messiest food spills. When it comes to designing a kitchen, one of the first design decisions is whether to replace countertops and cabinets or refurbish the existing ones. Cost is always a consideration, and we should also be concerned about limiting waste and reusing wherever and whatever we can.

Refurbish What You Have

Using existing counters and refurbishing them by covering them with recycled materials on your own is the greenest choice of all.

The Perils of Stone

Brand new countertops of Carrara marble—the medium of choice for Da Vinci and Michelangelo—are beautiful but come at a high cost. The marble is quarried from deep in the earth and shipped around the world, so it has a large carbon footprint as well as a steep price tag. Granite is likewise both expensive and nonrenewable, since once marble and granite are quarried they are not easily replaced. But even if you reject natural stone like marble and granite, you can still have beautiful countertops while being more green.

Top-Notch New Countertops

Newer countertops, available in composite slabs, generally fall into two main categories: paper and resin composites, and recycled glass and concrete.

Since I like the look of a poured cement countertop but don't like the environmental costs of cement production, I was delighted to find a countertop made from postconsumer waste, recycled paper, and petroleum-free resins. PaperStone, manufactured in the United States, is durable, eco-friendly, and certified by groups like the Rainforest Alliance and the Forest Stewardship Council, which rigorously monitor how the materials that go into such products are harvested. Other paper and resin options for eco-friendly counter surfaces are made by Richlite and Shetka Stone.

If you are drawn to the recycled glass and concrete compositions, check out manufacturers like EnviroGLAS, IceStone, Trinity Glass, and Vetrazzo, many of which use recycled curbside glass in their products.

ABOVE: I covered these basic wood countertops with linoleum tiles and protected them with polyurethane finish. This was a stylish solution—and inexpensive, at a total cost of only $74! In the same kitchen I also used wainscoting panels to give cabinets a fresh look loaded with charm.

OPPOSITE PAGE: These PaperStone countertops are made from recycled paper but certainly look chic. The combination of Energy Star appliances and vintage items makes this one very green kitchen!

This multipurpose wood table provides seating for as many as eight and extends the work surface for a busy chef.

If you install new cabinetry, consider a plate rack, an old but good idea that's recently come back in style.

RIGHT: A unifying coat of off-white paint shows off the lovely glass doors on these cabinets. Butcher block countertops can be eco-friendly—just look for trustworthy sources.

OPPOSITE PAGE: A stainless steel table from a kitchen supply store provides extra counter space and fits seamlessly into a room that wears its vintage fixtures proudly.

Use low-VOC polyurethanes and stains on wooden countertops.

For those seeking a modern look, recycled aluminum countertops are available from companies like Eleek and Alkemi, which use aluminum scrap and resins to create a durable and reflective material.

Wood or butcher block-type counters are a perennial favorite. Companies like Craft-Art and Endura offer both reclaimed wood and certified wood products to ensure that the materials used in their countertops are not drawn from nonsustainable sources.

KITCHEN ISLANDS

Islands are one of the best ways to expand counter space in an older kitchen while reusing interesting materials. First determine where you want the island to go and then choose objects to repurpose for the shape, height, and style you want. Whether you use it for food prep, impromptu guest seating, extra storage, or even the kids' homework, think out of the box when it comes to finding your own private island.

Island Shopping, or How to Find a New (Old) Kitchen Island

☞ Decide what the island will be used for most: do you want it to accommodate stools, or will it be used for food prep?

☞ Measure, measure, measure before shopping. I always carry the measurements of things I'm on the lookout for, since I never know when or where I'll find them.

☞ Although you should have an idea of the style you want—rustic, modern, traditional—be open to new looks.

☞ Decide whether you want the piece to be static or movable.

☞ Once you've determined the basic requirements, go shopping! Flea markets, thrift stores, kitchen supply stores, eBay, craigslist (http://www.craigslist.org/), and garage and stoop sales are all great resources.

☞ Consider unusual pieces to fill the island role: stainless steel tables, vintage dining room side boards, workshop or library tables, midcentury credenzas— anything that has the right footprint and proper height for kitchen duty.

☞ Pieces you love can be altered: attach heavy-duty wheels; cut marble remnants or wood blocks to size.

ABOVE: Quality lives! This bar from the eighteenth century works beautifully as a twenty-first-century kitchen island.

RIGHT: Beadboard makes a lovely base for islands in these country kitchens.

FIXTURES

Nothing can compare to a deep, enameled farm sink, often divided and big enough to accept the largest roaster or pot. Repurposed kitchen sinks are made well and offer quite a cost savings.

If you're installing a new kitchen sink, consider adding a flow control aerator, which will enable you to direct the flow from the faucet as well as control water flow. An aerator reduces water use by 50 percent by mixing water with air, and it has a minimal effect on water pressure. By saving about 280 gallons a month for each faucet, you can lower your water bill and preserve natural resources.

BACKSPLASHES

Recycled glass tiles are the current darlings of every kitchen redo. Though obviously green, they come at a premium cost. Nonrecycled glass tiles are an option, but they will not only be produced from new glass but may also be shipped from far-flung locales. You could take a page from some of the decorator shows on television and create your own mosaic backsplash with broken pottery or glass shards. I've used recycled materials like beadboard and tin ceiling panels for some of my kitchen renovations.

RIGHT: My small city kitchen got a shot in the arm with a recycled glass backsplash and beadboard cabinets. The beadboard here is new, but I've often used salvaged board with great success. Notice the unadorned kitchen window. **OPPOSITE PAGE, CLOCKWISE FROM LEFT:** This beautiful porcelain sink was salvaged locally, so its green cred is unimpeachable! ❀ Old sink, classic style. Capture the vintage look with the convenience of the new, perhaps dressed up with a skirt made of gingham. ❀ I salvaged this classic enamel farm sink and love its streamlined good looks and pure white color. Since there are separate taps for hot and cold, I plug up the drain and run both taps to get the perfect temperature. ❀ A vintage porcelain sink rests on a simple, handmade hardwood base. The streamlined base and contemporary gooseneck faucet give it a modern look.

For a post-decoration photograph of this kitchen, see page 65.

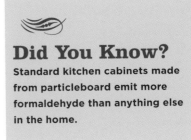

Did You Know?
Standard kitchen cabinets made from particleboard emit more formaldehyde than anything else in the home.

LEFT: Old cabinets, sans doors. Open fronts and a fresh coat of paint create a new look.
OPPOSITE PAGE: Here's a case where existing cabinets can be saved and reused. These contribute to the base of what can be an interesting kitchen island.

KITCHEN CABINETS AND STORAGE
Refacing Cabinets

New kitchen cabinets are awfully expensive. Anyone who has ever demolished a kitchen knows that those old kitchen cabinets are destined for the landfill. Instead of spending big bucks and filling up the nearest dump, reface your cabinets with recycled materials. For several kitchen remodels I've done,

Tips for Using Existing Cabinets

☞ Replace existing hardware and update with a different look; if you had brass before, try stainless. You can often find repurposed handles, pulls, and hinges at salvage yards.

☞ A few coats of VOC-free paint will give your cabinets a fresh, new look. Remove the doors and hardware for best results, sand surfaces to prepare for painting, and then give cabinets and doors multiple coats of paint. (For painting tips see page 109.)

☞ Replace the cabinet doors with vintage doors, windows, repurposed paneling, or other salvaged materials.

☞ For a totally different look, simply remove doors and use cabinets as open shelving. This look works best for someone who keeps things organized and objects that look good exposed, such as stacks of matching tableware, shelves of neatly organized spices, or pretty colored glassware.

☞ If you decide to go doorless, line the cabinets with a patterned wallpaper. Papering the back wall is all you need to do for instant impact. Cheerful stripes or bold flowers can bring just the right amount of pop to an otherwise neutral palette.

Remember to use art in the kitchen. I adore art with food themes, like this old apple carton label.

I've left the cabinets intact and simply changed out the cabinet doors. You can put material such as wainscoting directly over the existing doors, or replace them with reconfigured things like old windows. Multiple coats of paint help unify the look. You can even give repurposed cabinetry a modern edge by using up-to-date materials, such as brushed stainless steel, for the hardware.

REPLACING CABINETS

If those kitchen cabinets just have to go, remove them intact if you can, and consider donating them to a charity like the Salvation Army or Goodwill or selling them on craigslist so they have a chance for a new life.

Vintage ceramic bowls make great accessories, especially when you find them in colors that match your scheme. The blue stripe in this bowl picks up on the wall color.

LEFT: With these new cabinets, I went for a vintage look with beadboard and insisted on purchasing from a supplier that uses recycled, low-VOC particleboard and low-formaldehyde manufacturing.
OPPOSITE PAGE: "As is" has its charms, as with the greenish blue finish of the upper cabinet and the primitive look of the peeling cabinet beneath it.

Vintage glass is always in style, in a decorative collection or hard at work on the family table.

Brand new cabinets are expensive and may also contain hardwoods, lumber from old-growth forests, or toxic glues and adhesives; on top of all that, they may have traveled great distances to reach you. Before you lay your money down, consider some alternatives.

Open Shelving

Open shelving is one option we're seeing a lot of these days. You can install open shelves where the upper cabinets used to be for a streamlined look on a streamlined budget. Choose woods that were obtained responsibly, or better yet, use salvaged wood.

New Cabinets Can Be Eco-Friendly

If you're buying new, keep an eye out for cabinets made with sustainable materials and processes.

☞ Renewable, FSC-certified, or salvaged wood is better than particleboard or fiberboard. Another alternative is sustainable wheatboard, now available from many manufacturers.

☞ Finishes, paints, and adhesives should be nontoxic.

☞ Manufacturing processes should be formaldehyde-free.

☞ Finishes and composite products like particleboard should emit few or no VOCs.

LEFT: New cabinets that house dishes and collectibles have vintage appeal when details like crown molding are included.
OPPOSITE PAGE: Open shelving works well in both contemporary and country-style interiors. These shelves beautifully display a lifetime collection of vintage glassware.

Vintage Furnishings

Who says kitchens have to have built-in cabinets? Any flea market, or even a well-stocked thrift store, will have multiple choices when it comes to china cabinets, credenzas, solid bookcases, and even old secretaries. Think out of the box and think paint! Look for sturdy pieces with wide doors and stable shelves that can take a daily pounding. You could even get a couple of pieces from a similar era—say 1950s Formica with sliding glass front doors for a modern look, or carved Mediterranean for a rustic theme. A well-built credenza makes a great kitchen counter, with storage for pots and pans below and even drawers for silverware and utensils. Simply made pieces in pine, oak, or maple work seamlessly with new or old appliances and are in ample supply at nearly any country flea market.

White bowls, pottery, and pitchers can regularly be found at flea markets and antique stores. A collection of silver spoons complements the dishes.

Third Place Green

Using vintage pieces to decorate is the ultimate when it comes to living sustainably. Why not use vintage tableware, such as china, utensils, and glassware? If you can't find entire place settings, mix and match for added charm. You needn't buy expensive antiques. Check out your local thrift store; the variety available is awesome.

Second Place Silver

Since kitchens are the scene of so much family time, it's important to make sure that the lightbulbs used there are compact fluorescents. You can mitigate the glare of these bulbs by using candles at mealtime for a warming glow. When I was a kid, candles meant it was a special occasion; why not make every evening special? And consider using soy rather that paraffin candles, since the latter are made using a by-product of the fuel refining process.

First Place Gold

Sometimes that refrigerator just has to go, and with the Energy Star products available today, replacing an old appliance can be a smart move. Instead of buying a brand new (and expensive) stainless steel refrigerator, consider a "gently used" one. An increasing number of organizations are offering perfectly good appliances that have been demoed from high-end remodeling jobs, giving you a chance to get that coveted six-burner chef's stove at a fraction of the original price (nice!) while reducing the impact on our landfills (nicer!). An article in *The New York Times* cites some places that offer salvaged appliances:

- **In New York, New York:** Build it Green! (http://www.bignyc.org/)
- **In Barnegat, New Jersey:** Recycling the Past (http://www.recyclingthepast.com/)
- **In Chicago, Illinois:** Island Girl Salvage (http://www.islandgirlsalvage.com/), Murco Recycling Enterprises Inc. (http://www.murco.net/)
- **In Palo Alto, California:** Driftwood Salvage (http://www.driftwoodsalvage.com/)

ABOVE: A round pedestal table with six mismatched chairs is the perfect place for family meals and card games.

OPPOSITE PAGE: The beautiful floors in this kitchen were made from salvaged, wide-planked wood.

A FEW WORDS ABOUT KITCHEN FLOORS

Remember when hardwood floors in kitchens were rare and choosing a kitchen floor meant picking one of five colors of linoleum? Those days are long gone, although linoleum, either newly installed or preserved, remains an option. Today, if you want to install new kitchen floors with an eye toward being green, you have several choices.

Reclaimed Wood

Trees that have fallen naturally due to storm or age and wood salvaged from razed structures are considered reclaimed materials. I like reclaimed wood because of the warmth that it has developed from age and the character bestowed by nails and years of wear and tear.

Renewable Woods

As discussed in the entryway chapter, renewable woods like bamboo, cork, and eucalyptus mature quickly and are considered renewable. Just keep in mind that the location from which your floor material is shipped should be part of the equation. Bamboo shipped from foreign countries or even across the United States has a much bigger carbon footprint than local maple or oak.

Tiered cake plates and baskets make great, displayable storage for fruits and vegetables, candies, or other family treats. The chandelier was rescued from a thrift store and outfitted with CFL bulbs.

Concrete

Concrete floors and countertops are currently all the rage. They can be easily customized with stains and have a polished modern look. Concrete can be relatively inexpensive to install, especially if the kitchen already contains an existing layer of concrete subflooring. Concrete's manufacturing process, however, creates large quantities of carbon dioxide; one source suggests that 7 percent of global CO_2 emissions come from concrete. Hydrochloric acid is typically used as the base for concrete stain, but there are eco-friendly solutions available, like low-VOC acid-free soy-based stains. Check out Eco-Safety Products (http://www.ecoprocote.com/) if you're considering concrete floors and want to pursue some sustainable options.

Stone

As with countertops, natural stone makes for a gorgeous floor, but some choices are greener than others. Marble and granite are the least eco-friendly because deep excavation and shipping from foreign countries contribute to CO_2 emissions. Local stone that has been salvaged from existing installations can be a green choice, but it will probably cost you dearly. Slate and sandstone lie

ABOVE: Who knew linoleum was eco-friendly? It's a product derived from linseed oil and continues—much like it did in the 1950s—to make smashing floors.
OPPOSITE PAGE: The large-scale squares of natural stone make this country kitchen a standout. All of the furnishings, cabinets, and appliances are vintage.

closer to the earth's surface and can be more efficiently mined, but still require excavation that causes environmental pollution.

Linoleum

Many people don't know that linoleum is a natural product made from linseed oil solids. I often find perfectly intact linoleum floors in the kitchens I renovate, proof of the product's durability. If installed using adhesives with little or no off-gassing, linoleum is considered a sustainable material. Just ask the manufacturer what types of low-VOC adhesives will work with linoleum. As with paint, water-based adhesives have lower emissions than do solvent-based versions. The important thing to remember is that not all adhesives work for all materials, and it's best to ask the floor manufacturer which adhesive will work with its product.

Marmoleum

A composite of linseed oil, rosins, and wood flour, marmoleum looks like lino-leum but comes in an astounding—and modern—selection of colors.

Recycled Rubber

A large selection of recycled rubber is available in tiles or rolls. This material is both durable and comfortable to stand on for long periods of time. According to HGTV's Web site, rubber flooring has the same price point as linoleum,

Grandmother's Tip

Fashions come and go, hemlines rise and fall, but one thing has remained constant in my life: my grandmother's innate sense of sustainable living. If she gave a hoot about what other people think, right about now she'd be saying, "I told you so." From gardening to canning, from table scraps to composting, from reusing kitchen foil to collecting rainwater, my grandmother is the original Ed Begley, Jr. Here are some of grandmother's tips for life in the heart of her house, the kitchen!

☞ If you have the real estate—or even a terrace or window sill—don't buy it, grow it. My grandmother not only canned all kinds of vegetables and fruit, she grew what she canned in her own garden.

☞ Along with reusing aluminum foil, my grandmother repurposed plastic bread bags to use instead of sandwich bags, and instead of paper towels, she used pure cotton or linen towels.

☞ Be on the lookout for hardware you can recycle from furniture that you might not otherwise use. I can't tell you how many drawer pulls and cabinet handles I've removed from furniture put out on the sidewalk for trash.

approximately $3 to $5 per square foot installed. Expanko's Reztec Rubber Flooring (http://www.expanko.com/) makes a variety of rubber flooring options.

Rugs

What better place for a cheery recycled braided rug than in the kitchen? Made from scraps of wool, denim, or toweling, braided rugs are durable, charming, and 100 percent recycled. You'll find them at flea markets or "new" on the Internet—or you can even braid your own.

FURNISHINGS FIT FOR A KITCHEN

Many of today's new kitchens now include the dining room, and even residents of older homes are razing walls to combine these once separate rooms. Since I've always favored a less formal arrangement for family meals, this softening of the boundaries between two distinct rooms is welcome, but it does raise the question of how and where to sit.

Vintage containers add considerable charm; I don't mind that this canister got separated from its mates!

KITCHEN APPLIANCE CAVEAT

Most home cooks want the latest chef's stove and a stainless steel refrigerator, and there's nothing like sleek new appliances to transform a kitchen, but a few of my remodeled kitchens feature vintage appliances, like big enameled ovens from the 1940s and '50s and even one bulbous fridge I just couldn't part with. They're energy-guzzlers when compared with modern appliances, but I love their stylized look, and I'd rather see them standing proudly in my kitchen than lying in a dump.

If you're shopping for brand new appliances, "vintage style" pieces will give your remodeled kitchen a warmer look. Whether you purchase the latest stainless steel appliances or new ones designed to look old, make sure you look for the Energy Star label to get a product that is as energy-efficient as possible.

ACCESSORIES

It's tough for me to walk through a flea market or thrift store and leave empty-handed. Large glass jars, the simpler the better, make great canisters for family necessities like flour, sugar, and salt. Who doesn't need an extra

Did You Know?

According to the Aluminum Association, Americans throw away enough aluminum every three months to rebuild the commercial air fleet. If you can't get out of the aluminum foil habit, buy 100 percent recycled aluminum foil. Give a quick rinse to the foil you've used and toss it in with the aluminum cans going out for recycling.

OPPOSITE PAGE: Even though vintage appliances are energy hogs, they may be suitable for a country home used only seasonally, and they certainly look better here than in the landfill!

tray or serving platter? I can't resist accessorizing directly from the flea market table to mine: whether it's a collection of colorful ceramic roosters to perch on the counter or a large wooden pepper mill, nearly all of my kitchen goods were bought used. That goes for artwork, too. Don't be afraid to hang art in the kitchen, especially if your kitchen and family room run seamlessly together. I love to hang primitive paintings or food-related drawings in and around the kitchen, particularly near seating areas.

RIGHT: This vintage Wedgewood stove's classic lines are hard to resist.

OPPOSITE PAGE: Although this might not be a favorite option for bachelorettes or empty-nesters, a picnic table is a fine solution for a growing family.

Old flour or feed sacks made of cotton or linen make wonderful pillows for an otherwise hard seat. Fill them with cotton batting or even strips of your old denim jeans!

— Menu —
Manchego & Roasted Red Pepper Toasts
Grilled Shrimp & Avocado
Tomato & Corn Salad
Cucumber & Dill Salad
Sliced Beets & Fresh Mozzarella

Peach & Raspberry Pie

You'll appreciate kitchen accessories all the more if they are both functional and pretty.

WINDOW TREATMENTS

I prefer to keep kitchen windows unadorned when privacy is not an issue. Natural sunlight keeps heating costs down, and nothing feels better than the sun streaming in on a clear fall day. If privacy matters, try installing repurposed wooden shutters on the inside! You'll find lots of choices at country flea markets—the more primitive the better. Sometimes I even leave them just as I found them if they have an aged patina.

LIGHTING

Every kitchen I've designed has a repurposed chandelier. From crystal and confection to plain brass to wrought iron, I'm always on the lookout for chandeliers wherever I go. Lighting is something that gets changed out frequently, and someone else's fancy last year may be yours today, or vice versa. Don't forget to use CFL bulbs!

LEFT: When it comes to chandeliers, purchase locally. Your corner thrift store or antique shop is sure to have a few options. Remove or add shades, paint or embellish, and turn nondescript lighting into high-wattage chic.

OPPOSITE PAGE, CLOCKWISE FROM TOP LEFT: A simple chalkboard makes a fun—and useful—accessory for the kitchen. ❀ Natural bamboo shades are a versatile solution when you want the option of privacy. The natural texture and color of these shades complement a wide range of styles, from contemporary to simple country. ❀ These fine vintage accessories are perfect for the modern kitchen.

Living Rooms
RELAX INTO YOUR SURROUNDINGS

Three different prints and four different fabrics were used on these upholstered pieces. A color palette of chocolate brown, white, and lime green tied them all together. By varying the prints—such as a large floral (sofa), a small print (chairs), and a graphic print (ottoman)—you can create an updated look even on traditional pieces. Throw in a solid (lime green tufted chair in corner) and a stripe (pillows on sofa) and it somehow all comes together. **ABOVE:** The classic shape of this table lamp appealed to me; I paired it with a black shade for extra drama. The other decorative objects are vintage, as is the carved mirror.

I ONCE BOUGHT A PIECE OF COUNTRY PROPERTY THAT CAME with an old house. I passed by that house every time I visited my place in the country, and one day I saw a caretaker mowing the lawn, so I stopped to ask him if the place was for sale. The owners wanted to sell, but the historic nature of the place, coupled with its dilapidated state and proximity to an old cemetery, meant there were few takers. I must admit that I was smitten with the grounds, with their commanding view and nearby stream, and the sagging house was merely an afterthought, but when I walked the property, my eye kept returning to the house and its worn profile, to the patches of blue sky showing through where they shouldn't: windows out, chunks of roof missing.

Pull the curtains back and let the breeze in to cool a room.

The house was too far gone to save and refurbish, but I used every bit of it in other places I was renovating. Much as a mother hands down a cherished string of pearls, that house gave me stair railings and wide, worn planks for flooring, wainscoting and decorative molding, doorknobs and other hardware, and the magnificent beams that reach across the ceiling of a brand new living room, taking the edge off its newness, grounding it, and passing on a sense of permanence.

Although modern living rooms have a few major appliances that guzzle energy, such as the wide-screen high-definition televisions, gaming systems, and surround sound, it's still possible to achieve a sense of tranquility inspired by eco-friendly, green materials. The pages that follow focus less on these modern amusements and more on the seating arrangements and furnishings. From fabrics to floor coverings and from paints to furniture, living rooms can truly be a thoughtful exercise in living sustainably.

OPPOSITE PAGE: From the natural textured rug to the vintage furnishings to the salvaged wood beam, everything in this living room adds up to a place of tranquility and peace where residents can unwind.

Notice my grandmother's door snakes used to conserve heat. Take a look at page 85, top photo, for this decorated room.

FLOORING

Living rooms should be warm, comfortable, and inviting, and though you may not consciously notice it, what's underfoot contributes a great deal to the feeling of a room. Whether covered in warm wood, textured sisal, natural-dyed kilims, worn Oriental carpets, good old country braided rugs, or paint, a floor can create a mood from the bottom up.

Wood Floors

All hardwood floors should be made from material that was sustainably grown or harvested, or salvaged or repurposed. We wouldn't dream of cutting down old growth sequoias in the Redwood National Park, which is home to some of the oldest trees on the planet. Some are estimated to be 2,000 years old. Many people still want redwood floors because the wood is durable, slow to decay, and beautiful, so an ideal source is second growth sequoias harvested from managed forests. The key is management, and a trustworthy source for determining that timber was harvested from a well-managed forest is the Forest Stewardship Council. We can also use salvaged woods from demolished buildings and trees that have fallen naturally. Not only does some wood age beautifully, but reusing the wood from an old barn or from a razed house provides a sense of pride, not to mention a fabulous anecdote for any cocktail party.

I repurposed the knotty pine floor boards from a razed house for living room floors in a new construction, and I couldn't be happier with the results. If you don't have an extra house or barn to raze for repurposed wood, look for distributors of salvaged wood. It doesn't come cheap, but nothing beats the warmth, patina, and character of wood that's lived several different lives. If you decide to purchase salvaged wood from a dealer, try to acquire it from a nearby sources and avoid long-distance shipping. Ask the dealer where the wood came from; if it's traveled far, its large carbon footprint mitigates the fact that it was salvaged.

Another option for sustainable wood floors, along with bamboo (which was discussed in the entryway chapter), is eucalyptus, a quick-growing wood that should be purchased from manufacturers who can certify eco-friendly harvesting.

Floor Covering

Standard carpeting made of nylon, acrylic, or polyester has a synthetic backing containing, among other things, petroleum. All of these materials emit gases, a process known as off-gassing. Rugs and carpeting made from wool,

The natural color of this rug creates a neutral base for the room.

ABOVE: There's a reason sisal rugs are all the rage: they look great, they're affordable, and it's easy to harvest the fibers sustainably.

OPPOSITE PAGE: Using salvaged wood for floors gives a big payoff, both for the beauty of the room and the security of the environment.

BELOW: This luxurious wool carpet in my city apartment keeps things cozy.

BELOW: This luxurious wool carpet in my city apartment keeps things cozy.

OPPOSITE PAGE: This chair evokes memories of a cherished relative, so it's definitely a keeper. The ottoman would make a great do-it-yourself upholstery project.

cotton, silk, sisal, jute, seagrass, bamboo, and other natural fibers are available to those who prefer to avoid using synthetic materials in their homes. For carpeting to be truly eco-friendly, the materials and production must be free of pesticides, food additives, and chemical treatments (including those that make them fire retardant) and made from resources that were harvested sustainably and ethically. While it may be difficult and expensive to be absolutely certain that carpeting is produced sustainably, some basic considerations will help you get the healthiest options.

✣ Consider wool carpeting (from farms that follow ethical practices for raising and tending sheep) rather than synthetic, since it's stronger and more stain and mildew resistant.

Third Place Green

Instead of buying a new piece of furniture for the living room, rearrange what you already have. You'll be surprised how fresh an old familiar piece will look in a different location. Don't make the rookie mistake of throwing all the furniture against the wall. Angle a cabinet in the corner, or position the sofa in the center of the room with a narrow table behind it stacked with books. It's only furniture! You can always move it back. Also think about balancing the height of the furnishings in the room. All low-slung furniture up against the wall will look odd whether you have tall ceilings or not. Put a tall piece—say a bookcase or standing lamp—in a corner, or flank a low credenza with two tall pieces. Try different arrangements, and you'll know when you have a winner.

Second Place Silver

Re-cover that favorite chair in vintage fabric. You'll need five or six yards of material to cover the average club chair. Between flea markets, thrift stores, and eBay, you can lay your hands on some great fabrics. Consider it vintage if it's material from the 1930s, '40s, or '50s; fabric through the '80s is sometimes called collectible. You can get remnants from an upholsterer or fabric shop. Don't be afraid to mix and match. If you don't have quite enough, use two coordinating fabrics. Try a pattern and stripe; just make sure they both contain a matching hue.

First Place Gold

Save an item that's headed for the landfill and repurpose it for your living room instead. Check with friends and neighbors to see whether they have items that are headed for the sidewalk or the nearest dumpster. If the piece is sturdy and you like the design, averting its trip to the landfill is both eco-friendly and thrifty.

✧ Find out what material the carpet backing is made of and look for materials that are petrochemical free.

✧ Don't forget about the location of the manufacturer, since the energy used to ship products long distances can mitigate all the good you're doing by purchasing natural fibers and low- or no-chemical additives.

FURNISHINGS

I love choosing furniture—the big ticket items—for the living room. These are big decisions, and figuring out color and pattern should involve some thought, but I stay open to serendipity as I explore flea markets, thrift stores, and garage

sales. I've found Berger chairs in the French style and midcentury American club chairs. I almost hate buying a sofa, because I know there's an even cooler one right around the next corner. There is simply too much great stuff out there, most of it more stylish, better made, and cheaper than any of the brand new items on the market. Keep the following thoughts in mind whenever you shop for living room furniture.

→ Look for sofas and chairs in classic designs. Straight and modern, English-inspired, or camelback, with a tufted back or studded with nails, even a Louis XV has a timeless appeal that works in almost any room.

Take a good look at the quality of the wood and check for damaged sections. It won't be worth it to reupholster unless the frame is blemish free.

→ Consider sofas with a little bit of leg, as opposed to the big block of upholstery flush to the floor.

→ Ottomans are versatile pieces that can extend a sofa or chair or fill in as coffee tables. They are also less expensive to reupholster than larger pieces and may even make a good do-it-yourself project.

→ Vintage sofas with three or four front legs are a real find because they often represent superior craftsmanship.

→ I like to mix some pieces that have external, sometimes ornate, wood frames with all-upholstered pieces. I paint the wood frames either black or white to give them an edge. (If the fabric needs refreshing you can add a bright modern color or graphic.)

→ Remove the seat cushions from upholstered pieces before you buy and look at the manufacturer's label, which will cite place of origin and material content. Many pieces crafted in North Carolina in the past fifty years are quite well made. Labels will also indicate fabric and stuffing content. I always prefer cotton, linen, and silk for upholstery fabric; cotton or wool down-filled cushions are a mark of high quality.

Reupholstered Furnishings

Imagine the impact on the nation's landfills if we recast the large upholstered furnishings that we need throughout our lives. Give grandmother's sturdy

ABOVE: The sturdy bones of this regal seat deserve a good upholsterer and a second life. **OPPOSITE PAGE, CLOCKWISE FROM TOP:** Don't think that the fabric on your upholstered pieces has to match. Mix it up so that your living room is truly individual, not some version of a furniture showroom. ❖ If the cushion of your favorite leather chair has cracked, consider swapping in an upholstered seat rather than tossing the chair. ❖ Gingham was a bold choice for this sofa. The secret to using pattern on a large upholstered piece is to link it together with other items in the room (like the wallpaper and the throw) through color.

wood-frame sofa a second act with snazzy new ticking or faux zebra stripe upholstery, and then a third act with the wood frame painted white and the fabric replaced with heavy cotton canvas.

I've had the good fortune to come across a talented upholsterer, who is right up there with my family doctor in terms of valued relationships. (I even send him a holiday card!) Good upholstery services are expensive, but so are brand new sofas and chairs, and reupholstering is always better for the environment than buying new; even purchasing new eco-friendly furnishings is not as green as reusing existing items. Remember too that a good upholsterer can offer you hundreds of choices of fabrics, many of them organic. Even the best stores only offer a limited range of fabrics on new pieces of furniture.

Vintage stoneware and glasses make for attractive display pieces and can be puchased inexpensively at any thrift or antique store.

There's a difference between reupholstering and re-covering. The former entails refurbishing the piece from the frame up, replacing webbing, springs, filling, and cushioning, as well as the fabric, which is the most expensive. Maybe you can get away with simply re-covering that favorite chair with fresh new fabric.

Between the labor and the fabric, what's worth the expense of reupholstering?

❖ Items with sturdy, well-made frames of kiln-dried hardwood (oak, maple, ash, or mahogany) will last for a long time, justifying the investment in new upholstery.

❖ Pieces you love and that can't be replaced are worth keeping for their sentimental value.

❖ Hang on to period pieces that are well made and perfectly suited to your design scheme or the space in which you plan to use them.

Repurpose big-ticket items like sofas, chairs, storage, and side tables; buy vintage and paint (everything looks good in black or white!) or have big pieces re-covered. If new is what you need, consider pieces made from sustainable wood and shipped from North Carolina—a center for American-made furniture—rather than flown in from Mexico or China.

OPPOSITE PAGE: An Empire-style sofa was covered in a bold stripe. Although this piece was used in a fairly traditional design scheme, it would also work well with contemporary, deco, or 1950s pieces.

If you have the luxury of double-wide doorjambs, French doors are de rigueur.

HEARTH AND HOME

Although wood-burning fireplaces and stoves aren't always energy-efficient, the actual burning of wood is considered carbon neutral, since no more CO_2 is released than if the wood were to degrade naturally in the forest. Woodheat (http://www.woodheat.org/) is a great place to learn about making your wood-burning fireplace eco-friendly.

As far as decorating, a fireplace is prime real estate for the singular adornment that a wonderful old mantel can provide. A mantel can display your collections or serve as a sculptural piece on its own. If a house comes with a mantel of any interest, refurbish or reuse it; if it doesn't, hunt down a replacement at country flea markets or auctions.

LEFT: This terrific mantel, an auction find, goes beautifully with the locally quarried bluestone of the hearth.

OPPOSITE PAGE, CLOCKWISE FROM TOP LEFT: A screen installed over the radiator allows heat circulation, while built-in cabinets made of salvaged wood provide storage. This is a great use of space that would otherwise be wasted because of the radiator's footprint. ❋ This wood-burning stove isn't old, but repurposed ceiling tins make a handsome—and heatproof—backdrop for the vent. ❋ Use what you find. This savvy homeowner found a great old mantel, but it was too large for the hearth. He decided to use it anyway and create extra storage in the bargain. ❋ Purchased from the construction site of a New York townhouse, this black carved mantel, left in its original state, is clearly the focal point in the room.

ACCESSORIES

One of the easiest and most enjoyable ways to accessorize is to use vintage items. Hunting and gathering at flea markets, thrift stores, and antique shops is part of what makes the decorating process so enjoyable. Keep an eye out for these used and repurposable living room accessories.

→ Interesting picture frames can vary widely in shape and material, suiting any décor.

→ Architectural and ornamental pieces can be hung on the wall or used as bookends. Iron gates, wooden molds, and old tools look great when gathered in a collection on the wall or on a shelf.

→ Can you have too many mirrors? Look for those with beveled edges, ornate frames, and varying shapes. Don't be shy about grouping three or more together for a big impact.

RIGHT: A burled wood tray creates an impromptu coffee table when paired with a tufted ottoman. It's the perfect place for vintage plated silver— probably hotel silver from the 1940s or '50s.

OPPOSITE PAGE: Searching for amber glassware makes my flea market trips more fun, and my kids love getting involved in the scavenger hunt. The single-hued collection creates a lovely visual effect.

Vintage pitchers go the distance as a cache for utensils or flowers or even to serve lemonade.

✤ Pick a color and start collecting glass vases, bowls, or pitchers. Mix squat and thin, short and tall.

STORE IT!

Lately I've been paring down, creating simpler tableaus, and making sure that each piece of furniture or accessory I choose earns its keep. Storage becomes important when you're going for a streamlined look. In the living room, look for pieces that hold a lot, aren't too fussy, and are flexible enough to transition into the next decorating scheme that's decades away. Keep an eye out for these vintage storage options.

✤ Multiple sets of bookcases can be used separately in small places or lined up together to create a wall of storage.

BELOW, LEFT: This collection of vintage glassware is in shades of blue.

BELOW, RIGHT: Employ different materials for their texture as well as their color. Metal and wood, produce and fabric all come together to make a compelling still life.

OPPOSITE PAGE: The only thing more satisfying than hunting for the vintage accessories that fill the shelves of this bookcase is knowing that I've saved them from the landfill.

LEFT: Repurpose wood buffet tables into skinny side tables under windows or in hallways.
OPPOSITE PAGE: Country saws, complete with a patina of rust, make curious art. Just make sure they're hung securely!

✢ Vintage credenzas often have solid doors behind which to hide detritus.

✢ Solid, well-designed sideboards or dining room cabinets can be painted or left as is and used as living room storage.

✢ Some ottomans have removable tops and can double as a hidden cache for pillows or throws.

✢ Chests or trunks can double as coffee or side tables.

✢ Carved wood, fabric, mosaic, tin, or Bakelite or lucite boxes can be stacked on shelves or under tables.

✢ Custom-made shelving is wonderful if it has a small footprint and a clean, modern design. Use repurposed or sustainable woods and VOC-free laminates in construction.

TREAT YOUR WINDOWS

Window treatments are like ties and necklaces, giving the outfit—or, in this case, the room—the desired air of formality, casualness, or something in between. Unless you're a member of the royal family or were lucky enough to be born into the landed gentry, windows swaddled with heavy silk or damask draperies and embellished with valances or swags seem over the top. Simple lines, easy fabrics, subtle hues, sustainable materials, and utter utility feel good and look good in almost any setting. Curtains should close without a lot of fuss; blinds should go up and down easily. Light can then let in or kept out depending on the need.

Carve out space for a cozy window seat and take advantage of the natural light to read a book or newspaper.

TOP LEFT: These wooden shutters have striking straight architectural lines; they're also a lot easier to maintain than delicate fabrics.

BOTTOM LEFT: These filmy sheers offer privacy when needed and allow in filtered light even when drawn. I hung them as high as possible to draw the eye up.

OPPOSITE PAGE, RIGHT: Wooden shutters as a window treatment in the living room have a clean-edged look with great appeal.

OPPOSITE PAGE, LEFT: A window seat provides extra storage in this country living room.

OPPOSITE PAGE: Lamps are crucial for proper reading light. Swap in a CFL bulb for green cred.

There's an unlimited variety of fabric for window treatments, but making a sustainable choice takes a little research. Natural materials like silk, linen, cotton, and bamboo are lovely, but certified organic choices are very expensive. If chemicals—like fire retardants—are added to fabric then the material is probably no longer considered organic, but remember how important fire retardation is, especially in a child's room.

While the idea of organic fabric appeals to me, a strict "organics-only" policy is tough to live up to. I opt for vintage fabrics or all-cotton canvas drop cloths from the big box store instead, incorporating sustainable design solutions while staying within a budget.

No matter what sort of fabric you choose, try to hang curtains as high as possible and make sure they fall to the floor for a more streamlined look that will make the ceiling look taller.

Wood or aluminum blinds, plantation shutters, and matchstick or roller shades can be a crisp and efficient alternative to fabric. I've always been a fan of the simple, white roller shade, which is cheap and works in both rustic and modern décor.

Keeping the blinds drawn in the summer will keep the space cooler, with less need for air-conditioning. In the winter, I use sheer curtains to let in the most sunlight during the day, and draw the heavier curtains at night to retain the room's heat.

LIGHTING

Table lamps create a beautiful ambient light. Look for lamps with classic or interesting shapes, since wood and even metal can be painted. Check out fixtures that could be transformed with shades, new globes, or a fresh coat of paint. CFL bulbs used throughout the living room are money-savers in the long run, and much better for the environment. Manufacturers are also paying attention to consumer needs by producing bulbs that emit a softer, less glaring light.

The lamp may be brand new, but the feeling is vintage, circa 1960!

A chandelier in the bedroom
is a nice touch, especially
when it adds a bit
of Hollywood glam.

Bedrooms

GREEN DREAMS

Repurposing furnishings, lighting, linens, and decorative items in such a thoughtful way makes a welcoming and eco-friendly statement. **ABOVE:** Vintage iron bedframes are plentiful and perfect for guest and children's bedrooms.

BEDROOM'S ARE PERHAPS THE MOST PERSONAL ROOMS IN the home; just walking into a bedroom should fill you with a sense of calm and well-being. By keeping the design scheme simple and adding a few creature comforts, your bedroom can be a rejuvenating oasis that prepares you for your next busy day. With a little forethought about finishes and material content, you can also reduce the allergens and toxicity in the air for a better night's sleep. The bedroom can be a relatively easy, inexpensive, and fun decorating project for a beginning designer, since there are no expensive fixtures to deal with and many decorating props can be vintage.

RIGHT: The small footprint of a demilune table is perfect between two beds.

OPPOSITE PAGE: This regal mirror takes pride of place as a headboard. Its fragile silvering and the vintage bed linens all create a feeling of stolen afternoons in days gone by.

Even though this house is brand new, the repurposed furnishings lend it an air of permanence. This vintage mantle came from a construction site and remains in its natural state, sans paint.

Choosing no-VOC paints and finishes for these walls helped make this bedroom an inspired retreat.

WALLS

Paint is one of the easiest and most economical ways to change the feel of a room. Volatile organic compounds can cause headaches, dizziness, and asthma attacks; fortunately, low- and no-VOC paint is available in a large and growing number of colors. Although low-VOC paints are a little more expensive and may require a few extra coats, they can certainly be worth the time and money, especially in the bedroom.

FLOORS

Getting out of bed in the morning is surely more pleasant when there's a soft rug underfoot. Since most bedrooms are relatively small, they may be the place to spend a few extra dollars and indulge in organic natural fibers.

Rugs and carpeting are often crafted from organic materials such as hand-sheared, vegetable-dyed wools and bamboo-cotton-hemp-sisal blends. Natural-content rugs offer benefits over synthetic materials like nylon. Wool is quite durable and contains lanolin, which makes it naturally resistant to stains. Be aware that many wool rugs and carpets are treated with chemicals in order to make them resistant to stains and fire, so ask about this before purchasing.

Many vintage and semiantique rugs were made with pure wool and/or silk and cotton blends, making them an excellent choice for the bedroom. If they need cleaning, look for dry cleaners that offer nontoxic cleaning processes such as wet cleaning with biodegradable detergents or a technology developed under contract with the EPA that uses recaptured liquid carbon dioxide. You can also rent a steam cleaner and fill it with plain water rather than harsh chemicals.

Painted floors are an eco-friendly way to freshen up old wood floors without replacing them.

If your hardwood floors have seen better days, instead of installing wall-to-wall carpeting or purchasing new area rugs, put down a few coats of paint. I like white or gray porch paint for a country look, and several low-VOC versions are available. Just give the floors a light sanding and be prepared to lay on primer and multiple coats of paint. You can finish with a low-VOC lacquer finish to protect your handiwork. Remember VOC-free paints don't give off

Painting Smart

Here are some tips for painting green, even if you paint the room blue.

☞ If you don't use VOC-free paints, use latex-based rather than oil-based paints.

☞ Carefully calculate the right amount of paint for the job so you don't buy more paint than you need. One gallon should cover approximately 350 sq. feet.

☞ Use low- or no-VOC paint thinners and strippers.

☞ Don't expose yourself or your family members, especially children, to lead paint, which was used in most homes and even on furniture built prior to 1978.

☞ Seal leftover paint cans tightly with plastic wrap, make sure the metal lids fit securely over the plastic, and then turn the cans upside down. The seal is airtight and keeps paint fresh.

OPPOSITE PAGE: This collectible needlepoint rug fills in for artwork and works well with the cannonball-style headboard. Look for new versions of this traditional design manufactured in sustainable woods.

harmful gasses, so *always* use them. (You can get VOC-free paints at big-box stores like Home Depot or at any specialty paint store.)

FURNISHING FAVORITES
Vintage Beds

Once while traveling in Europe, I stayed at an old hotel. The big antique bed, made of dark, carved wood, stood so high off the floor that a small footstool was provided to make the climb easier. I've never slept better than I did that night, and I continue to search for an antique bedstead that is as solid as the Great Wall of China.

RIGHT: A braided rug is a savvy choice for this country bedroom.
OPPOSITE PAGE, TOP: This beautiful antique bed is a real showpiece. The inlaid floral designs on the headboard and footboard echo the swirling pattern on the frosted French doors.
OPPOSITE PAGE, BOTTOM: Whether you load the bed with pillows and layers of linen or keep it spare and neat, iron bedsteads are beyond the trends. Big or small, doubles or twins, iron beds will outlive us all; now that's sustainable!

Frosted glass doors allow sunlight in while still allowing for privacy.

Tips for Buying Vintage Beds

☞ Measure the space where the bed will go and carry measurements with you to flea markets and auctions.

☞ When purchasing an entire bedstead at a flea market, ask to see the bed put together to make sure that all the pieces fit and nothing is missing.

☞ Even though vintage pieces may come in unconventional sizes or have missing pieces, don't dismiss them. You can have rails made or look for replacements in thrift stores.

☞ Standard queen- and king-size mattresses were not introduced in this country until the 1950s, so most vintage or antique bed frames are singles or fulls. These old double frames work great in the guest room or second bedroom.

☞ Never use a vintage crib or bedstead with chipped paint for infants or very young children; older cribs don't have the safety features of new ones, and peeling paint will most likely contain lead.

☞ Remember the scale of the room and other furnishings when choosing a bed frame. Massive headboards or tall canopy beds will overwhelm a small bedroom.

☞ If a wooden headboard seems dark and gloomy, imagine it in a coat of paint.

They don't make beds like they used to. Vintage head- and footboards are sturdy and have timeless appeal. Finding the perfect design for the modern bedroom isn't always easy and you may have to have a mattress custom made for an odd-sized old bed, but the quality and uniqueness outweigh the disadvantages. Tall people like me can save money by skipping the footboard—also a good look if the room is on the small side.

Remember those 1950s sitcoms where the bedrooms of married couples featured matching twin beds? I say bring back the twin bedstead, not necessarily in the master bedroom, but in the second bedroom, guestroom, or child's room.

Don't let a bad finish stand in the way of a sale; most vintage headboards can be given a bright new one. Wood or metal pieces can be painted white or ebonized for a modern look, and if you find a frame that features flat panels on the head or footboard, you could even apply wallpaper, a decoupage collage, or nifty vintage fabric.

Dressers and Such

My solution for storing clothes in the bedroom usually involves a trip to the Salvation Army to pick up a sturdy dresser. You can pay a fortune for a brand new piece of furniture from a manufacturer, or you can go to one of the big-box stores sprouting up across the country for some "bargain" furnishings made from particleboard, but those are lose-lose propositions. Why pay a fortune for solid wood when you can get it for a fraction of the cost in vintage? That particleboard dresser may look appealing now, but how long will the drawers run smoothly? Particleboard is also made from pressed wood and usually contains off-gassing formaldehyde, not something you want in the bedroom.

The bed frames match, so the bedding doesn't have to.

Look for sturdy dressers made entirely of wood, including the back, and drawers held together by tongue-and-groove carpentry, not glue. Don't worry about the finish or the drawer pulls because you can change all that. I like dressers with deep, all-wood drawers that glide back and forth effortlessly. (You can sand the runners and then rub bar soap on them if the drawers stick.) Stand back and take a good hard look at the piece you're considering. Will the basic design work in the room in which it will be used? Carved

ABOVE: Paint somehow makes this grand old dresser less fussy. I would use a piece like this in a small bedroom but keep the rest of the look minimal. The horizontal wood siding and bare plank floors also contribute to the fresh, casual look.

OPPOSITE PAGE, CLOCKWISE FROM TOP: These twin brass and iron beds would make any kid's room fun! ❀ For a tiny city bedroom and a growing family, two upholstered, crib-sized sleigh-style beds were a great solution for a tight spot. When outgrown by their users, the beds could be re-covered for a new pair of siblings or even used as additional seating in a more spacious living room. ❀ Matching twin headboards in an enigmatic style—British Colonial? Regency?—make terrific guest room accommodations.

Nothing beats the versatility of a vintage trunk: it's furniture plus storage.

detailing and bow-front drawers add distinctive styling but may not work in a room where you want a simpler look. Choose a dresser that is stable, well constructed, and pleasing to the eye, and you will have it for many years to come.

A reading chair, a tiny side table, a bench at the end of the bed for doffing shoes: these are the things that give a bedroom the creature comforts that we all crave at the end of a hard day. By mostly purchasing vintage or "gently used" items, I can sometimes splurge on something brand new, like a tufted armchair with matching ottoman, crafted of sustainable woods and organic fabrics. If you've done your part for the planet by repurposing many furnishings and fixtures, you can probably rationalize buying one or two new pieces, especially if they were made with eco-friendly materials and processes.

ABOVE, FROM LEFT: Simple is more in this cozy guest room. ❈ An old dining room cabinet makes a great place to store linens; you could even remove the doors.
OPPOSITE PAGE: If you've got the room, add a trunk, bench, basket, or box at the foot of the bed to store linens, pillows, quilts, and other necessities.

ACCESSORIES

Before choosing a mattress, do some research. Conventional mattresses may contain petrochemical-laced vinyl coverings, softeners such as phthalates (an EPA-recognized carcinogen), polyurethane foam that emits VOCs, and potentially toxic chemical fire retardants like polybromenated diphenyl etners (PBDEs), according to Healthy Child, Healthy World, an LA-based nonprofit dedicated to raising awareness about environmental issues that affect children. Some mattresses are labeled "organic," but while portions of the mattress may contain organic fibers, the United States Department of Agriculture (USDA) certification standards are so stringent—taking into account everything from soil content to pesticides to fiber content and from handling to processing to manufacturing—that a 100 percent USDA-certified organic mattress probably

RIGHT: Open shelving can be decorative when linens and bed clothes are kept as neat as a pin. I love the mixed textures of the baskets.

OPPOSITE PAGE, CLOCKWISE FROM LEFT: This chair gets more comfortable when you know it's made of 100 percent recycled wire. ❁ This lime green chair was crafted of sustainable wood and covered with organic fabrics. The wrought iron side table and artwork are also vintage. ❁ Old handkerchiefs make excellent— and unique—pillowcases. ❁ Old game boards make great accessories for your child's room.

Before you toss that old drawer,
try replacing its pulls with
vintage hardware for a new look.

When decorating a tight city bedroom, my grandmother's advice echoed in the back of my mind: "Mirrors make a small space seem bigger." once again, she was right.

ABOVE: A pale green dresser acts as both clothing storage and bedside table. Notice how the color is picked up in both the bed linens and the artwork.
RIGHT: In my apartment, rather than having permanent bookcases made, I opted for floor-to-ceiling bookcases that can be removed and taken with us or repositioned when the urge to redecorate takes hold.

Third Place Green

It's not always easy to outfit an entire room in vintage furnishings. If you have your heart set on a certain queen-size bed frame in the British Colonial style, go ahead and splurge. If not, look for new furniture made from FSC-certified sustainable wood.

Second Place Silver

When replacing large items like mattresses, practice due diligence and recycle. Some charities accept mattress donations for resale or recycling. For example, Goodwill Industries dismantles mattresses, separates each layer, and sends the foam to carpet makers, the wood frames to paper mills, and the cotton to filter manufacturers. The steel springs go to an auto recycler, a solution they're hoping to refine since it remains cost-prohibitive.

First Place Gold

With a good ceiling fan and a fair crosswind from the open windows, you just might be able to forgo air-conditioning in the bedroom. The atmosphere will benefit from fewer greenhouse gas emissions, and you may be surprised by how much it reduces your electric bill.

ABOVE, LEFT: This dark dresser may be scuffed, but that adds rustic charm. It's all wood and as strong as an ox.

ABOVE, RIGHT: The old twin iron bedsteads of my forebears were part of my childhood, and I've made them a part of my kids' lives, too.

OPPOSITE PAGE: A bed dressed with freshly laundered antique linen is the ultimate luxury.

doesn't exist. Beds and bedding advertised as organic probably contain minimal chemicals and toxins and use natural materials like organic cotton and wool, horsehair, mohair, alpaca, hemp, bamboo, and rubber. If you aspire to as organic a mattress as possible and are ready to take the plunge, here are a few things to keep in mind.

→ Look for a mattress free of PBDEs.

→ Avoid purchasing mattresses with foam interiors that contain petroleum products.

→ Flame-resistant barriers made of fiber in the mattress are better for your health than sprayed-on fire-resistant chemicals.

→ Look for coverings made of organic cotton or wool rather than vinyl.

→ If you can't afford one of the high-priced organic mattresses, consider purchasing an organic encasement in order to put a layer between you and any potential toxins.

You might be surprised to know that solidly made single-paned glass holds in just as much heat as new double-paned when matched with an equally-strong storm window.

BED LINENS

By dressing your bed in organic or vintage linens, you're taking another step toward sustainable living. Sheets, pillowcases, and comforters made from organic cotton and other natural materials are readily available. Organic products are more expensive, but compared to some other high-priced items like appliances and new flooring, organic bedding may be considered an affordable luxury.

BELOW: Vintage linen and fabrics look good rolled and layered if you've got the space to display them openly.

RIGHT: A mixture of vintage linen and new organic cotton makes this particular bed a thoughtful combination of comfort and sustainability.

OPPOSITE PAGE: Small vintage lamp bases can be scooped up at second-hand shops for a few dollars. In this guest room, a vintage lamp makes the perfect bedside light. The iron bedstead, side table, and clothing rack are also vintage.

Even a headboard without its matching
footboard and rails can usually be
married to a standard modern bed frame
if it's attached to the wall.

LIGHTING

Multipurpose lighting in the bedroom is a must. Reading in bed calls for direct, bright light, handy enough to turn on and off without getting up. As a potential setting for romance, discreet and soft lighting should also be an option. Any flea market or thrift store will have many examples of diminutive lamps from the 1940s; they usually come in pairs (or used to) and are made of milk glass, marble, or alabaster. While probably too small for bedside reading lights, they make great mood lighting for that other favorite bedtime activity. Another option is the dimmer switch for overhead lights, which is famously simple to install and provides a lot of bang for the buck.

RIGHT: Lamps on either side make for happy bedtime readers. During the day with the curtains open, this makes a cozy spot for reading by natural light.

OPPOSITE PAGE: Rattan roll-down shades work well in this simple country bedroom.

In a tight spot? Consider a floor lamp and forget the table.

TREATING BEDROOM WINDOWS

Since the bedroom is the home's true sanctuary, it goes without saying that the window treatments found there must not only control light but offer privacy. Consider curtains, blinds, and shades made from organic fabrics, bamboo, or other sustainable materials; they can let in sunlight to warm the room in winter and block it in summer to reduce the need for air-conditioning and fans.

If you choose sustainable materials like bamboo, hemp, silk, flax, or other natural plant fibers for window coverings, take the green quotient one step further by making sure that toxic pesticides and chemicals were not used in

Salvage and repurpose tables, such as these on either side of the bed, for a stylish air.

their growth or manufacture. Synthetic dyes and fire retardants contain chemicals that emit toxic fumes. Since consumers can't always count on in-store labeling of organic textiles, one way to reliably find chemical-free fabrics is through the Internet, from companies that are dedicated to eco-friendly products.

LET'S CLEAR THE AIR

Perhaps more than other room, the bedroom cries out for clean air. Air purifiers are popular, but there is scant evidence that they relieve the symptoms of asthma or allergies. Some purifiers even emit ozone into the air in the process of supposedly cleaning it, according to Consumer Reports.

The EPA has a few simple rules for keeping indoor air quality as high as possible.

→ Eliminate the source of air pollutants inside the bedroom. Don't smoke, burn candles or incense, or use air fresheners, and keep pets out of the bedroom. Vacuum often.

→ Improve ventilation by keeping windows and the bedroom door open when possible. Use outdoor-venting fans and keep air conditioner filters clean.

Plants can be a beautiful addition to a room as long as they are healthy and well maintained. Areca and bamboo palms, peace lilies, Boston ferns, English ivy, Janet Craig dracaena, and rubber trees produce oxygen and may even remove toxins from the air. If you have pets, especially cats, ask your veterinarian and plant supplier which plants are nontoxic to animals.

Grandmother's Tip

During the dog days of summer, all the window shades in my grandmother's house were drawn tight to keep out the fierce rays of the sun, while windows were left open to let in a breeze. The house stayed amazingly cool.

Bathrooms

BATHED IN GREEN

Sweet retreat! An ample tub to stretch and soak in; immortal stone to gird one's dreams; an airy chamber with room to ruminate—can restoration be far behind? **ABOVE:** Repurposed beadboard paneling, fancy sconces, and a cast-iron sink with fluted column together make salvage chic.

BACK WHEN WE WERE KIDS, BEFORE THE NOSTALGIA KICKED in, we weren't so keen about my grandmother's frugal ways. Take bath time. The huge, claw-foot tub in her bathroom just begged to be filled to the brim for a long, luxurious soak. Not on grandmother's watch! We got an inch of tepid water, maybe two, and up until we were tweens we bathed together. It was her way of saving that precious farmer's resource: water. We didn't know it then, but grandmother's obsession with saving water was way ahead of its time.

Just like the kitchen, the bathroom is one of the first places homeowners want to renovate, and it's an excellent room to focus on when you want to reduce a family's impact on the environment. (In the long run, being a little more resourceful in the bathroom can save money, too.) Bathrooms are open to a range of eco-friendly designs and renovations. From purchasing biodegradable cleaning products and certified organic towels to incorporating a vintage sink or bathtub that otherwise might be headed for the landfill or installing new water-saving fixtures and recycled glass tiles, creating a more sustainable bathroom can help make the planet more green.

WALLS AND FLOORS

While new floors, walls, and bath surrounds are usually part of a bathroom renovation, consider where that demoed material ends up after removal. In an older home, consider keeping intact tile as is if you can live with the color. Ceramic tile can be pulverized and recycled, but so much of the detritus pulled out for a bathroom renovation ends up in the garbage and ultimately in a landfill.

Replacing Tile

If you decide that the old tile just has to go, redo the walls and floors with recycled tiles or sustainable natural materials. Natural stone like marble, granite, or even slate is both expensive and environmentally damaging. Consider some of the following options instead.

Decorative tin—or possibly faux-
tin—ceiling panels running halfway
up the walls add old-world charm.

Recycled ceramic tiles: Made from postindustrial recycled and other raw materials, these are the low-cost winners.

Recycled glass tiles: Made from recycled bottles, recycled glass is an eco-friendly choice but does have certain limitations. It can be slippery when wet, so the best choice for floors is a tile that has a sand-blasted surface. Adhesives will be visible beneath the glass if not installed properly using the right fixative, so glass tiles should only be put in by an experienced installer.

Keeping Demoed Tile Out of the Landfill

☛ Remove ceramic tiles with care, clean off the mortar, and reuse them.

☛ Use broken pieces of tile in a mosaic.

☛ Donate tile to a salvage outfit.

☛ Collect smaller broken bits to use as gravel or drainage in the bottom of houseplant pots.

Recycled metal tiles: Tiles made from recycled brass and aluminum are beautiful but should only be used on walls or as floor accents, since they get very slippery.

Hardwood: You can use hardwood in the bathroom if it is treated with multiple coats of polyurethane and resealed once a year.

Rubber: Available in both rolls and tiles, recycled rubber is great in the bathroom since it resists mildew and mold, and when waxed periodically can be cleaned with soap and water.

Find storage wherever you can. This nook houses towels and bath salts.

Beautifying Walls

Walls can be paneled or papered if the ventilation is adequate; I love beadboard paneling in a country bathroom. Any of the tiling options mentioned in the floor section can also be used on walls. Materials like recycled glass and recycled aluminum work well on walls where the slipperiness of the surface is not an issue.

SINKS

Old pedestal sinks have real weight and presence. When resurfacing these salvaged beauties, I make sure to use low- or no-VOC finishes. Sometimes I just use them as is and let their chipped and gently used finishes speak for themselves. Don't pass on a pedestal sink just because you don't like the look of the base or the pipes underneath: you can always cover it up with a skirt.

Turning Taps

Many old faucets have separate spigots for hot and cold, and I've been known to keep them intact. Instead of running water down the drain while you wash, put in the stopper and fill the basin with hot and cold water from both taps. The result is just enough water at just the right temperature, with a smaller waste stream!

Some faucets and taps do need to be replaced, and the older faucets really do release much more water than newer, more efficient models. When replacing

ABOVE: Turned sideways with fixtures mounted on the wall, this claw-foot beauty becomes sculpture in its on right.

OPPOSITE PAGE: A new pedestal sink of this size and quality would be expensive to replace and lack the character of this weighty version from the 1920s. How many children learned to brush their teeth here? How many young men took their first shave? These relics remind us of those who came before, and isn't there value in holding onto that?

ABOVE, CLOCKWISE FROM RIGHT: This glass-fronted cabinet makes a great place to stow towels and linens. Its location in the hallway maximizes bathroom real estate. ❀ This pleated skirt hides a multitude of sins, from ugly pipes to unsightly storage. ❀ A vintage Carrara marble sink is married to an antique table for a one-of-a-kind vanity. ❀ Another clever modification of a vintage dresser, this time housing double sinks.

OPPOSITE PAGE: Notice the stark contrast between the white ceramic sink and the dark wood vanity it is built into.

Saving the home's original stained-glass window is an act of eco-friendly love, especially if the exterior is fitted with double-paned glass for extra insulation.

faucets, investigate the possibility of installing low-flow faucet aerators, which release much less water. Water-saving showerheads are also a must.

Saving Fixtures, One Sink at a Time

Nearly every time I walk down the block in New York City, I see a demoed sink or even a bathtub sitting on the sidewalk. Those old porcelain fixtures were made to last, and even those that could use a bright new finish are usually worth salvaging. Pedestal sinks and claw-foot tubs fit right in with older houses and any sort of vintage décor, so keep an eye out on your next stroll.

RUB-A-DUB-TUBS

There's nothing quite so romantic as a claw-foot tub. These tubs represent the dying art of bath time as ritual. Filling one of these vintage vessels takes time and consumes a huge volume of water, but refitting them with shower heads means that water-saving showers are an option. Refinish a tub that has seen better days, or enclose its base completely in wainscoting, as I did in one renovation. That tub will get a lot more mileage in its new manifestation.

Did You Know?
According to the American Water Works Association, 26.7 percent of the water used daily in the typical single-family home is flushed down the toilet. Installing more efficient toilets can significantly reduce daily water use.

Linoleum is considered a natural product, since it's made from linseed oil. This bathroom features linoleum floors and a vintage braided rug.

LEFT: Underneath the wainscoting is a perfectly usable claw-foot tub with a surface that even I couldn't save. Wood and a fresh coat of paint gave it new life.
OPPOSITE PAGE: A weathered column stands in for a base in this country bathroom. The countertop is repurposed cypress.

RIGHT, TOP: A set of simple, Shaker-style hooks extends storage possibilities in this bathroom. Beadboard siding adds to the farmhouse theme.

RIGHT, BOTTOM: Many would have junked this graceful claw-foot beauty for a newer model, but not this savvy homeowner. The tight corner is the perfect place for a tub sans shower.

OPPOSITE PAGE: The only thing new about this bathroom still life is the stainless faucet and shower converter; the claw-foot tub, hanging soap dish, and unique combination shelf and towel rack are all vintage finds.

138

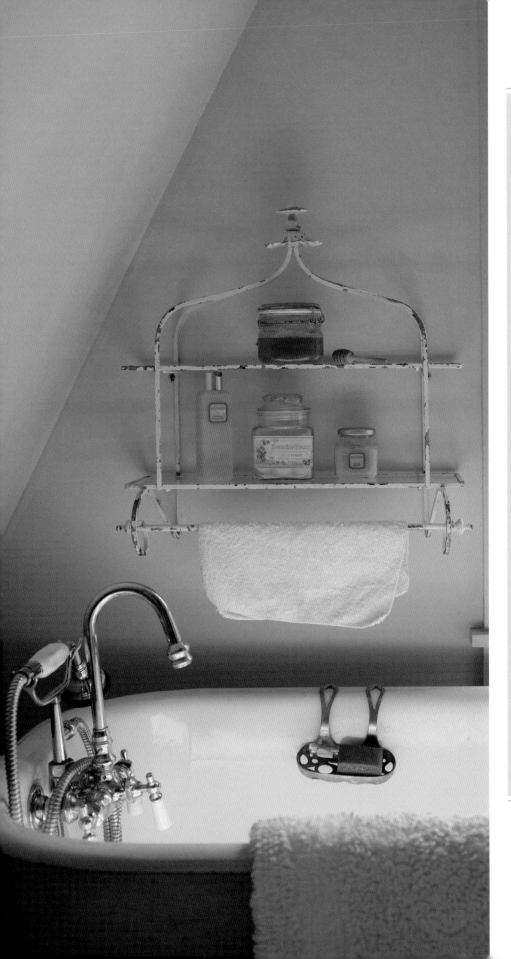

Third Place Green

When you renovate with recycled tiles, make sure to use low- or no-VOC adhesives and sealants that are made for the humid conditions of the bathroom.

Second Place Silver

If you love the look of handmade or custom tiles but can't afford them, use a few antique tiles as a design motif among the new. You can create a border or small focal point with the antique tile and use the new, noncustom tile around it.

First Place Gold

High-efficiency tankless water heaters, though initially more expensive, eventually pay for themselves in energy costs, which are up to 20 percent lower than those of traditional water heaters. Gas and electric tankless water heaters heat water more quickly than conventional gas-fired storage tank models and can thus save between $70 and $80 per year on fuel costs, according to Consumer Reports. Since tankless heaters are more than double the price of storage tank models, Consumer Reports also stated that it would take up to 22 years to break even.

A salvaged buffet/dining sideboard makes a great bathroom piece.

Refinishing Old Fixtures

You can save an older porcelain, fiberglass, or cast-iron tub or sink from the landfill by having it refinished, as long as the surface lacks holes or pits and is relatively smooth. It's a big job and involves caustic chemicals, but it can be done by a handy do-it-yourselfer or farmed out to an expert for $300 to $1000.

TOILETS

I don't reuse toilets—very few people do—but I do try to recycle them. Many recycling facilities crush porcelain toilets to make a concrete base for road construction. There are certainly advantages to using new toilets, the most important being that newer models use water much more efficiently. Depending on where you live, you may even be able to get an ultra-low-flush rebate from the local water company when you install a high-efficiency toilet.

ABOVE, FROM LEFT: This repurposed cabinet base provides a base for the sink, and sans drawers, it's perfect for shelving towels and linen. ❈ Shelves hung high in the corner increase storage, while vintage accessories like the oval mirror, urn, and leaded glass window treatment add charm.

OPPOSITE PAGE: Dark wood, salvaged fixtures, and clean, classical lines make this city bathroom a sophisticate's retreat. Note the old, high-level cistern toilet with overhead tank, which requires a pull of a chain to complete one's ablutions.

A tin ventilator edged in rust—perhaps from a barn or chicken coop—now tops this storage cabinet as impromptu sculpture. Be open to the artistic possibilities of ordinary or unusual objects.

MADE BY
UNO VENTILATOR CO
CLIFTONDALE, MASS.

According to the EPA, toilets in older homes should be replaced due to their inefficiency. The EPA recommends purchasing a toilet with the WaterSense program label, since these fixtures can save consumers up to 4,000 gallons of water annually and reduce water costs by more than $90 every year. Toilets that adhere to the WaterSense criteria come in a wide variety of styles and range in cost from fairly inexpensive to quite pricey.

FURNISHINGS AND STORAGE

The minimal real estate of most bathrooms means every item must serve a purpose. From cabinets that offer counter space and stow ample supplies to vanities that double as storage, everything must pull its weight.

Think out of the box when coming up with ideas for bathroom vanities, cabinets, and storage. Don't let provenance get in your way; just because a piece was originally designed for use in a living room or entryway doesn't mean it has to stay there. One person's medical cabinet becomes bathroom storage in its next lifetime. And why not reconstitute a Queen Anne nightstand as a vanity for a sink?

I also like to place unusual art in the bathroom. A valuable set of black-and-white photographs won't be able to withstand the humidity, but a small collection of flea market paintings—say primitive flowers—or framed photographs culled from some old issues of *National Geographic* would make great bathroom art. Another treatment that seems particularly bathroom appropriate is a wall of mirrors in frames of different shapes and sizes. If you don't require the extra storage that a medicine cabinet provides, consider removing it altogether and replacing it with a large and grand mirror, perhaps with a gilt frame or embellishments of seashells or collectible buttons. You can offer the cabinet to a needy friend and decorate the new mirror frame yourself for a fun project.

Grandmother's Tip

My grandmother wouldn't have dreamed of buying a fancy new bathroom wastebasket or special containers for cotton balls and other bathroom supplies. Find interesting old screw-top jars and cachepots from garage sales and thrift stores to house bathroom minutia. Buying brand new plastic containers makes no sense when there is an infinite supply of vintage containers available.

OPPOSITE PAGE: A primitive cabinet right outside the bathroom houses towels and linens.

The Home Office

WORKING WITH NATURE

Skip the ugly particleboard desks and workstations. In this town house, one entire portion of the room was designated the "office" by positioning a massive table made from reclaimed wood parallel to the bookshelves. **ABOVE:** Minimalism is the new black; less fuss, less muss.

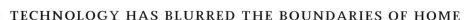

TECHNOLOGY HAS BLURRED THE BOUNDARIES OF HOME and office. Some sources say up to 80 percent of American homes have computers, and the list of devices that keep us connected to our jobs grows constantly. From those whose commute involves donning slippers and walking a few paces to those who simply use computers to pay bills and shop the Internet after working hours, many people see the appeal of a room or corner designated the home office.

FINDING SPACE

Homeowners and empty-nesters who are lucky enough to have an extra bedroom or finished basement can usually designate an entire room for the office. If you're not so fortunate, get creative. A closet without doors, a corner of the bedroom or kitchen, or even some square footage in the entryway or under stairs can be recast as an office space. A dining room table or kitchen island can fill in if you have a laptop and roll-away file cabinet.

RIGHT: A built-in counter takes up little real estate and provides ample space for two.

OPPOSITE PAGE, CLOCKWISE FROM TOP LEFT: This brand new armoire houses the computer and was even retrofitted with memo boards. You could get the same effect with a repurposed cabinet—although it would lack the sliding drawer for the keyboard—by drilling a hole in the back for cables. ❋ A slip of a space, the former closet, is enough for a desk, a chair, and a slimmed-down computer. Curtains provide a disappearing act at the end of a busy day. ❋ The library makes a traditional spot for a workspace, this one a simple table and chair. ❋ This ingenious homeowner carved out a niche for desk, storage, and chair in a space normally gone untapped: under the stairs.

My favorite object in this home is the table that converts into a place for a cozy supper for two.

OPPOSITE PAGE: An old clerk's workstation makes a fine place for homework or paying bills. Closing up the desk makes it easy to clear your mind of work-related thoughts.

DESK SET

The two most important elements in the home office are clearly the desk and chair. How much time you spend at your desk will dictate your choices here. If you spend a great deal of time online or at the computer, you'll need a proper desk or table and an ergonomic chair.

Be Seated

I hate the thought of an office chair in the bedroom or living room, but spending any length of time at a keyboard requires the support of a good chair. The variety of styles and colors available will help you find a chair that suits your physical needs as well as your vintage desk or table. With a top-of-the-line Herman Miller Aeron, Steelcase, Humanscale, or Neutral Posture chair, you will get beautifully designed seating—at a premium price—that will support your back and have a modern, even futuristic vibe that will work fine alongside a primitive wood farm table or polished glass. Like a good mattress, investment in a work chair is money well spent. If you're looking for eco- as well as ergo-, Steelcase says that its Think office chair is "99 percent recyclable by weight."

Make sure the desk and chair are at the ergonomically correct relative heights for your body shape. Test the comfort level of your workspace using an actual keyboard.

Working Surfaces

When I need a desk, I head to the thrift shop. First I check out the dining room tables, since there are usually lots of options. Look for long, narrow wood tables from the 1960s, rustic farm tables, glass tables on pedestals, or all white Saarinen-like tables that can pinch-hit as desks. Personally, I think long, rectangular shapes work better than round ones, but I would never turn down a Saarinen, fake or otherwise.

A wooden secretary is a sort of highboy cabinet with a compartment door that drops down flat to become the writing surface. Since secretaries have been out of fashion of late, I nearly always see at least one at every thrift shop I visit. It might not be ideal for someone who spends a lot of time working at home, but for bill-paying or the occasional Internet search, a secretary can do the job and seem fresh. Look for older ones made from solid wood and make sure the writing surface can support your laptop or monitor. Anything with a faux bamboo or Asian-inspired design would be fun, especially painted red, or you could buy something with classical lines and paint it glossy black. The key is to try to modernize the look a little.

BELOW: Bring back the secretary! They've been out of fashion since the advent of the personal computer, so you'll find loads of options at the thrift store.

OPPOSITE PAGE: A home office is where you can find it; one corner of this bedroom is enough for a small desk, a good light, and a sturdy chair.

You could also get a great-looking piece of salvaged wood, rustic but smooth, and pair it with a different style base or legs. A couple of two-drawer filing cabinets can act as both base and storage.

Don't forget the good old-fashioned wood desk. I still prefer narrow and long as opposed to chunky and square, but any desk made from solid wood and equipped with working drawers is a contender, since you can change out the hardware and paint.

This secretary fits perfectly into a cramped city apartment. Drop down the leaf, plug in the laptop, and voilà: instant office.

Third Place Green

Use a laptop rather than a desktop computer and save energy. According to multiple sources, laptops use 25 to 45 watts of electricity when running, compared to 60 to 250 watts for the average desktop computer.

Second Place Silver

Multitasking is good! Look for devices that serve more than one function. Printers with scanning and faxing capabilities use less energy and take up less space than multiple devices.

First Place Gold

Put down roots and take a bold step by creating a family heirloom. Instead of buying and throwing away particleboard desks as though they were tissues, get a solid desk that will last several lifetimes. A long, narrow Parsons-style table works well as a desk, and the closable writing surface of an old-fashioned secretary is great for those of us who aren't especially tidy. Your grandchildren will be glad to inherit your sturdy, beautiful office furniture.

BELOW: A humble little farmhouse table gets a new life as a place to pay bills, write letters, or prepare homework.
OPPOSITE PAGE, CLOCKWISE FROM LEFT: Wall sconces provide good directional light over a workstation that also includes superior storage in the built-in overhead shelves. ❀ Here a dining room table receives a second life as a sturdy office desk. I like the simplicity of the storage shelves paired with baskets for easy filing. Two retractable wall lamps provide ample lighting. ❀ During the day, with the blinds open, this work space gets great natural light. After hours, a desk lamp with an adjustable arm can be trained on intricate projects. ❀ Even an entryway table can convert into an impromptu office: with cleared tabletop, a laptop, and office supplies stowed below, this one becomes an instant workstation.

OFFICE LIGHTING

In the home office, I prefer table or floor lamps to overheads. While high-intensity halogen desk lamps seem to be all the rage, brass, ginger jar, or mercury glass vintage lamps with CFL bulbs trump new versions any day.

STORAGE

Even if much of the work you do is digital, you still need places to store the stuff that keeps the office running. Along with upgrading to the latest and smallest electronic devices, I like to keep my office space neat, with items I deem unattractive hidden away. Paper, envelopes, staplers, and ink cartridges all need to be housed somewhere, preferably out of sight.

Be open to new color possibilities wherever you find them. The color of this desk would be fabulous at a beach bungalow.

ABOVE: When "minimal" isn't your design ethos, you can still keep it orderly. Good design is all about editing. Every item in this handsome study carries its weight.

RIGHT: This closet is cleverly used to store office detritus. Shelves, covered boxes, and labels expand the use of the space and keep everything ordered.

OPPOSITE PAGE: Carve out space for a small workstation, like this traditional dark wood secretary.

Store It Beautifully!

If you can, designate a specific room or area as your office space and house all the materials and equipment that you need to work in that location.

Get a wireless router so you can put your desk anywhere you want and get online without trailing cable. Use a USB hub to manage electronic clutter. Antique drawers from furniture left on the street can house the glut of cables and power strips; drill holes or cut out a trench in the back of the drawer for the cables, and then stack them for a clean, unique look. If you're more the contemporary type, look for modern, specially designed boxes with cut-out cord trenches.

Make use of every inch of space. Hidden in the closet is the office's printer, file system, and Rolodex; a vertical luggage rack hangs on the door. The combination of the floral wallpaper, the collagelike bulletin board, and the tufted chair in this office creates a space where creativity can thrive.

Consider using a Parsons-style or other sleek table rather than a traditional desk for a cleaner look. Save surface space on vintage tables by installing a sliding keyboard drawer. Run cables along the underside of the desk rather than over the top. A two-drawer filing cabinet or storage caddy can hold supplies underneath the desk.

Use vintage wire or wooden in-boxes to keep bills and papers in order. If you have metal shelves or a metal desk, use small magnetic containers to house things like paper clips or display important memos. Collect pens and pencils in art pottery vases or scour European or Asian specialty food markets for canned goods with colorful, pop art labels; after you consume the mushy peas and quail eggs, you'll have a one-of-a-kind pencil caddy.

For a streamlined look, install wall shelves. Store office supplies in fabric-covered boxes, and supplement the effect with books, artifacts, and mementos. Surrounded by groups of books and other interesting finds on the shelves, computer equipment can be less oppressive and officelike. Also consider mounting the computer monitor on the wall.

Weather and time worked their magic on wood siding that covered a barn. Now this homeowner enjoys it every day since it's been brought indoors and repurposed as a beautiful wall covering.

ELECTRONIC DEVICES

Few things are as unattractive as a hulking computer monitor, or heaven forbid, a fax machine. While I'll never be labeled a techno-geek, I do applaud the downsizing of all manner of electronica, and wireless anything is a decorator's dream come true. Style is one thing certain tech manufacturers just get right, so banish the days when hardware needed to colonize the desk. A wireless keyboard, mouse, and printer will liberate your decorating psyche.

Energy-Efficient Gadgets

The simplest way to reduce energy waste is to look for the Energy Star label when purchasing home office products, from cordless phones to computers and printers to copiers and fax machines. Use Energy Star power adapters, which can be up to 30 percent more efficient, according to the DOE, and are often more compact and decorator friendly.

Most computers come with power-management features; use them. Low-power sleep modes simply mean that your monitors and computers go into hibernation—very low energy use—after a certain amount of inactivity. The sooner the unit hibernates, the more energy is saved.

Put all the devices you don't use at night, like the television, DVD player, and cell phone charger, on the same power strip, and turn it off before you go to bed.

Order printer cartridges online rather than driving to the store to pick them up. Better yet, learn to refill printer cartridges yourself to save money and the environment. Don't want to deal with the mess? Some retail outlets will refill your ink cartridges for you. Call to make sure they handle your model.

Print only what's absolutely necessary. Reuse paper by printing on both sides; for example, if you are printing out directions or a map, use the opposite side for a grocery list. Need I remind you to buy only 100 percent postconsumer recycled paper?

Use your computer like a filing cabinet and reduce the amount of waste you create. For example, if you need photographs of household items for insurance purposes, e-mail yourself digital versions; to reduce the amount of waste and keep them safe from fire or physical theft.

Did You Know?
According to the DOE, a computer that has a power-down or sleep mode will use 70 percent less energy than one without such power-management features. Make sure your computer is set to maximum energy savings.

OPPOSITE PAGE: Adopting this giant metal desk was an act of compassion. If you have the space, 1960s office goods are collectible and look good in any design scheme, whether cutting-edge or rustic.

Outdoors

IT'S GREEN OUTSIDE

It's hard to imagine our yards, porches, and entryways without a little greenery. **ABOVE:** A painted wood chair stands up to inclement weather and makes a useful perch for a plant.

ONE STEP OUTSIDE THE HOME AND ALL THE TALK ABOUT our environment takes on a feeling of immediacy. The house, apartment, condominium, or cabin is our shelter, but so is that canopy of trees, that cloudless sky, this patchwork carpet of grass and soil. The earth is our collective shelter and as its caretaker, our actions, large and small, really do matter.

YOUR HOME'S EXTERIOR

Of course we want the interior of our homes to be as healthy and comfortable as possible for the sake of our loved ones, but don't forget about the outside. The home's exterior paint, roofing, and landscaping all affect its occupants as well as the atmosphere we all share. Many brand new homes are being constructed with green manufacturing processes and materials, and many builders

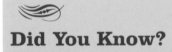

Did You Know?
According to HowToCompost.org, home composting can "divert 700 lbs. of material per household annually from the waste stream."

RIGHT: Plants outside the home are beautiful and smart: they help screen the sun and accessorize the exterior as well.

OPPOSITE PAGE: An old trestle table set under the arbor makes for great outdoor dining.

are interested in obtaining Leadership in Energy and Environmental Design (LEED) certification in new construction. Even existing homes can improve their carbon footprint in the course of making structural repairs. What follows are some of the ways a home's exterior can be tweaked to both save homeowners' dollars and be more sensitive to the environment.

Double-paned glass is a great insulator and will save money while raising your green quotient.

When replacing a roof, consider some of the new "cool" roofing material options like light-colored asphalt shingles, which reflect the sun's heat away from the roof. Metal shingles that have been treated with reflective coatings also deflect the sun's rays. Concrete and tile roofs can be installed with battens

RIGHT: Ivy hanging outside of this window creates a natural awning.
OPPOSITE PAGE: Plants, especially deciduous trees, are great for keeping interiors cooler during blazing summer months.

162

Encourage grass to grow between the bricks (instead of using mortar) for a dreamy walkway.

Third Place Green

Use vintage pieces for patio furniture. Old metal gliders dressed up with re-covered cushions can be oh-so-chic. Look for used rattan furniture in thrift stores and at flea markets. I like a mix-and-match look, coordinated by using vintage fabric for pillows and cushions. Side and coffee tables can be easily made from trunks, old leather suitcases, upended wooden barrels, and vintage wrought iron pieces. A piece of a thick tree trunk— naturally felled by a summer storm—makes a simple yet stunning side table.

Second Place Silver

Catch rainwater and use it to water plants, reducing your household waste stream. Just make sure to cover the receptacle with a very fine mesh screen to prevent mosquitoes from nesting.

First Place Gold

Forgo pesticides and commit to using organic fertilizers for lawn and plant care.

that form a gap between tile and roof; this creates ventilation that reduces the amount of heat retained in the attic, and thereby lowers cooling costs. Soffit vents admit air into the attic, extending the life of the roof, improving the circulation of hot air in winter months, and cooling the attic during the summer. For every soffit vent installed on the roof, there should be a roof vent or ridge vent. Additional information about energy-efficient roofing, especially on the West Coast, is available from the Cool Roof Rating Council (http://www.coolroofs.org/). Most of its members are roofing product manufacturers, but they claim to have a "fair, accurate and credible" rating system for more than 1,000 solar-reflecting and thermal-emitting roofing products in their Rated Products Directory.

An entire chapter could be devoted to the energy-saving properties, content, and installation of insulation. Nontoxic insulation with a high R-value (a measure of heat resistance) in the walls and roof will keep homes cooler in the summer and warmer in the winter.

Double-paned windows and tightly sealed exterior doors help keep the temperature where you want it without heating or air-conditioning. Every home can benefit from weather-stripping window and door frames, as well as sealing air conditioners and electrical, gas, cable, and telephone line points of entry. For thorough instructions on how to assess the home for air leaks and select and apply caulk or weather stripping, see the Weatherize Your Home fact sheet (http://www.pueblo.gsa.gov/cic_text/housing/weather/weather.htm/).

Exterior shades on east- and west-facing windows can reduce inside temperatures dramatically by blocking sunlight before it enters the home. Shade trees positioned southwest or southeast of a building also help keep interiors cooler in the summer; trees that lose their leaves in autumn are best, since they don't obstruct winter sun.

ENTERTAINING OUT-OF-DOORS

Gathering with friends and family for a splendid outdoor summer meal means turning off the air conditioner, setting out candles and tiki lights, and treating the patio like an extension of the living and dining rooms. Instead of paper plates or plastic utensils, proudly display your vintage finds: mismatched china cups, English place settings, pressed-glass goblets for homemade lemonade and sparkling rosé from a local vintner. Swathe the table in thrift store linen and give everyone cloth napkins. Dine on salads made from locally grown organic fruits and vegetables; grill kebabs and burgers made from free-range chickens and grass-fed cows.

These chairs may be too rustic inside, but they are perfect for outdoor eating.

ABOVE: Simple table and simple fare: simply satisfying.
OPPOSITE PAGE, CLOCKWISE FROM TOP: A makeshift drinks table out on the porch employs all vintage ware. ❖ An ironing board doesn't *have* to mean labor. Here it signifies fresh lemonade in pretty crystal glasses, which are much more fun than throw-away plastic. ❖ The light from these outdoor fixtures isn't too bright or harsh.

Get the kids involved by encouraging them to plan some good, old-fashioned fun! Swap electronic games, iPods, and cell phones for croquet matches, sack races, and a treasure hunt with a handmade map and clues.

LIGHT THE NIGHT

Along with tiki lights and soy candles, you might investigate solar-powered lights, which are now available in both decorative and spot varieties. Solar lights store energy from sunlight in rechargeable batteries. Since solar lights don't require wiring or access to the electric grid, many can simply be driven into the ground; every watt from the sun is savings on your electric bill.

Solars do have downsides. They need unobstructed sunlight throughout the day and even with full exposure, they may not be particularly bright. Many solar lights use nickel-cadmium batteries, which should be recycled rather than put into a landfill.

Fresh corn and the scent of flowers spell summer. Try growing a small garden— you won't regret reaping its rewards!

GROWING GREENER

From window boxes to vegetable patches, flower beds to herb gardens, growing something in the rich good earth brings satisfaction, beauty, and health. City dwellers need not despair; join a community garden for lush greenery and luscious tomatoes.

Home-grown vegetables and herbs simply taste better than store-bought varieties. Flowering plants and gardens bring a splash of color and beauty to a window box, yard, or city block. Oxygen-producing plants improve the atmosphere, and pesticide-free vegetables and herbs are good for you as well as delicious. It doesn't get more local than growing food yourself, significantly reducing your carbon footprint by removing the need to buy trucked-in or flown-in food.

ABOVE: Got a patch of land? Grow something!

OPPOSITE PAGE: From push lawn mowers to hedge clippers, models that use elbow grease rather than gas or electricity are much greener. Your neighbors will also love the fact that you're not making any annoying early morning noise! Keep hedges low to allow the afternoon sun in your windows.

No Pests, No Poison!

Here are a few tips for curbing pests without pesticides.

☞ Choose native and/or drought-tolerant plants that are best suited to the region. Their natural immunities make them better able to ward off local pests.

☞ Nutrient-rich compost grows stronger plants and helps them fight their natural predators.

☞ Rotate plants to allow soil to "rest."

☞ Consult with experts at your local gardening center to learn how plant diversity can discourage pests. Plants that resist insects are called resistant cultivars. A few examples include the Chinese holly rather than the Japanese holly, since the former resists the southern red mite; the male box elder rather than the female, since the male trees seem to ward off box elder pests; and herbs such as bay leaf, garlic, lavender, lemongrass, rosemary, spearmint, peppermint, and thyme.

"Plump up" the comfort factor of your vintage metal glider with solid seat cushions or loose back pillows.

COMPOST

No longer the sole province of hippie communes, composts are chic these days. Compost bins turn yard clippings, fallen leaves, newsprint, and ordinary table scraps and kitchen waste into rich fodder for the soil from which fantastic gardens grow. Even forward-thinking city dwellers are composting in cramped galley-style kitchens and donating their excess to community gardens.

Composting can also be a family activity. Get your children involved in deciding which kitchen scraps can go in the compost pile and let them turn the soil. It's a great hands-on way to teach kids about rejuvenating nature.

According to HowToCompost.org (http://www.howtocompost.org/), grass clippings, shredded leaves, vegetable peels, crushed eggshells, pine needles, wood ash, hair clippings, coffee grounds, and tea bags are ideal ingredients to add to your compost pile. Try to use a balanced mix of these materials. Never put in human or animal feces, cat litter, meat or fish scraps, or anything plastic or synthetic.

Turn and mix the pile twice a week to aerate it. Make sure the compost is damp—but not soaking wet—by adding water or using vegetable matter like lettuce and potato peelings. When the compost turns dark brown or black and looks like lumpy potting soil, it's ready to add to your garden soil.

OPPOSITE PAGE: The rewards of living green can be summed up here: enjoying the simple pleasures of a vintage glider now and knowing that this expansive rural greenery will be there for generations to come.

Living Green

AN ECO-FRIENDLY LIFE

Set out flowers with your dinner. Vintage pitcher optional. **ABOVE:** The worn columns, repurposed planters, and slightly "gone to seed" casualness of these plantings are a big sign of welcome that says, "Comfort lives here."

MY GRANDMOTHER PRESIDES OVER THIS BOOK IN MANY ways. As kids, my siblings and cousins and I cringed at her frugal ways, which we thought of as cheap. I now see them as groundbreaking. Her ideas of using just what you need, reusing anything that can do the same job over and over again, and repurposing things for a new task are concepts whose time has come. Rather than feeling cheap when I reuse something, I feel smart, and that feels good!

With a bucket of money, anyone can purchase sustainable goods and create an entirely green home from scratch. Very few people have the means to do this, however, and trashing everything to start anew would be tremendously wasteful. These three basic tenets of green redecorating will help you to balance budgetary and environmental needs.

Buy used: If you need something new, from silverware to sofas and from artwork to appliances, buy antique, vintage, or slightly used. Even if you need to refurbish it, the total cost will still likely be less than what you would pay for a new item.

Buy smart: If you must buy something new, then considerations such as energy efficiency, material content, construction process, and carbon footprint should take center stage.

Refuse to feed the landfill: Minimize the waste stream from your house to the landfill. Recycle glass, aluminum, paper, computers, batteries, lightbulbs, and hangers, even if it takes a little extra effort. Bigger items that still have life can be donated to thrift stores or charities, sold through craigslist or house and sidewalk sales, or simply offered to friends and neighbors. Imagine what a difference it would make if our sofas and armchairs found new life rather than spending their next life in the nearest dump.

SUSTAINABLE FOR THE HOLIDAYS

It's hard to resist a little indulgence around the holidays, especially when it comes to the people you love. But there's a lot we can do to minimize the

OPPOSITE PAGE: Me on a little green bench enjoying the outdoors. It's a pleasure I want my children to have, and their children, and their children's children.

Doormats are an important tool for keeping pesticides and chemicals outside.

environmental impact of the holidays that we enjoy throughout the year, without minimizing the fun.

OPPOSITE PAGE: Decorate your holiday table with wreaths and holly. Even without snow, things will look festive.

Winter Holidays

→ If you absolutely must decorate a Christmas tree, consider purchasing a live tree with its root-ball still attached so it can be planted afterward. Compost or mulch a live cut tree instead of putting it out with the trash.

→ LED holiday lights last about 200,000 hours and use 80 percent less electricity than incandescent lights. Solar Illuminations (http://www.solarilluminations.com/) stocks LED lights powered by solar panels.

→ Rather than burning paraffin candles, try beeswax or soy. Paraffin is produced from oil, so it adds far more pollutants to the air.

→ Forget expensive metallic gift wrap and use newsprint, old wallpaper, or old subway or highway maps. I love to use maps from *National Geographic*, which in the 1950s and '60s always contained a pullout map of some faraway place. Another option is a reusable gift bag.

→ Create holiday meals from 100 percent locally-grown products; it's a challenging but fun way to plan a feast. Prepare a menu (on recycled paper) that proudly informs your guests of your "buy local" theme.

→ Instead of buying new dinnerware or using paper plates, buy mismatched plates at the thrift store. After the party, donate them back.

→ American bittersweet, immediately identifiable by its bright red berry and yellow casing, is a popular decorating vine, but it is endangered in many regions and illegal to pick. Use commercially available oriental bittersweet instead. Just be careful not to allow birds or other wildlife access to it; as a nonnative plant, it will encroach on native species if given a chance to seed. Seal it in a plastic bag before disposing of it in the trash, or compost it after the holidays.

New Years

→ Planning a big party? Use e-mailed invitations rather than snail mail and reduce your carbon footprint!

→ Serve wine or bubbly from a local vineyard.

→ Make your own confetti from the paper shredder.

→ Use old tins filled with beans or river rocks for noisemakers.

The flag gate will look even better with a little wear and tear.

Valentine's Day

➔ Write an old-fashioned and from-the-heart poem to your sweetheart and make your own valentine card.

Look for vintage Valentine's Day cards at collectible shows or flea markets.

Fourth of July

➔ It's the easiest time of the year to plan outdoor activities, cutting back on air conditioner use and enjoying the freshness of summer.

➔ Use red, white, and blue cloth bunting instead of disposable paper products to create your Fourth of July theme party; you can store and reuse them next year.

ABOVE: Hurray for the red, white, and blue! Old Glory and a white picket fence: nothing could be more patriotic.

OPPOSITE PAGE: Autumn gourds and strings of chestnuts are an inexpensive and green decoration.

RIGHT: Amp up the modern country look with a movable display that changes seasonally. **OPPOSITE PAGE:** Reuse this leaf wreath again at Thanksgiving and Christmas.

Halloween

↷ Make your own masks with recycled paper bags or papier-mâché.

↷ Decorate with pumpkins, gourds, apples, fallen leaves, and other natural items that can be eaten or composted afterward.

↷ Use soy candles in those jack-o'-lanterns.

↷ Wean kids from the commercial candy habit; make your own caramel-covered apples, popcorn balls, or dried organic fruits.

SOME WORDS ABOUT RECYCLING

Recycling takes time. You need to learn how and what to recycle, and you have to integrate the habit of recycling into daily life, rinsing out containers and separating materials. Putting a few standardized props in place in your home will help make recycling second nature.

↷ Create designated bins for glass, metal, and paper recycling and put them in an accessible place in the kitchen or office.

↷ "Pre-cycle" by limiting the materials you bring into the home in the first place and making sure you buy items with recyclable packaging.

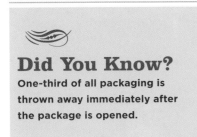

Did You Know?

One-third of all packaging is thrown away immediately after the package is opened.

Found art? Not exactly. But pumpkins, gourds, and other seasonal offerings make great impromptu sculpture.

+ Break the habit of single-use items and replace them with cloth cleaning rags, replaceable-blade razors, linen napkins, cloth diapers and hankies, and mesh coffee filters.

+ Get the whole family involved in recycling. Teach your kids about the process—or let them teach you!—and make recycling part of the discussion when you shop.

+ Purchase items made from recycled materials.

Most large cities and municipalities require residents to recycle and will collect recycling if it is separated properly. Check with the sanitation department in your area to find out what and how to recycle. The following are some basic guidelines.

+ **Paper and cardboard:** White and colored paper, envelopes, wrapping paper, smooth and corrugated cardboard, paper bags, newspapers, magazines, catalogs, phone books, and paperbacks can all be recycled. Staples are OK, but spiral bindings aren't. Paper that is soiled, glued, coated, or used for photography cannot be recycled and should be disposed of in the regular trash.

+ **Bottles, cans, and metal:** Metal aerosol, soup, pet food, and paint cans can all be recycled, as can aluminum foil and trays. Glass bottles and jars, plastic bottles and jugs, and milk and juice cartons can all be recycled, but caps and lids must be removed. Yogurt and deli containers should *not* be recycled. All material to be recycled should be clean.

You can also recycle wire hangers, tools, knives, or small appliances that are mostly metal.

Do not put auto batteries, fluorescent bulbs, thermometers, motor oil, paint, or tires in the recycling or the regular trash. These items are considered hazardous waste and must be disposed of separately. Most municipalities have special waste sites where residents can drop off such items.

ABOVE: Mismatched and vintage silverware from Goodwill can be polished and paired with china for large gatherings.
OPPOSITE PAGE: Floursack towels: the orginal recyclable. Our grandparents used these to fashion clothes, quilts, and linens.

Take care to display the red, white, and blue respectfully.

Conclusion
IN PRAISE OF LIVING SMALLER

We seem to constantly compare our possessions with those of our colleagues, neighbors, friends, and even family members. This becomes a no-win proposition, since there will always be someone else with something bigger and better. The movement to live more compatibly with our environment presents us with the opportunity to recast the American dream into a broader, more inclusive set of expectations that can satisfy our individual needs and goals while also honoring our place as global citizens.

Have you ever watched one of those reality shows in which a professional organizer visits a really messy person's home and helps that person bring order to the chaos? At the end of the show, there is inevitably a catharsis, when the resident, overwhelmed by the pristinely organized space, acknowledges that less is more, and that paring things down to some beautiful essentials is truly liberating. Although extreme, I think that's an example of what a little green consciousness can do for a home, a community, or even the planet.

The last thing that I want to do in this book is to come off as a scold, or as someone who is preaching about material abstinence or denial. I hope I have presented some tangible ways that environmentally sensitive decorating can satisfy our need to live in aesthetically pleasing surroundings. I think aesthetics and the environment are inextricably bound, so a single path can lead you to both good looks and eco-friendliness.

Picture an informal garden of native plants rather than exotic landscaping in pesticide-laced soil. Think smart bathrooms with water-saving toilets and repurposed claw-foot tubs rather than massive suites with seven water-gushing shower heads and Jacuzzis that are used once a year. Drive a pre-owned hybrid instead of a brand new souped-up SUV. Consider refurbishing

OPPOSITE PAGE: No McMansion here, but a simple, honest dignity. I love the wide-planked door and rough-hewn quality of this entryway.

that bungalow or colonial by taking down walls and reimagining the space before bulldozing and filling the acreage with a cavernous McMansion.

Smaller homes and living spaces can be truly liberating. Right out of the gate, a smaller home is less expensive to purchase or build. The money saved can go to upgrades in appliances and higher-quality materials. Smaller houses use less energy and therefore reduce energy bills. With less space to squander, you'll be more deliberate about the possessions you want to bring into that space.

Possessions have a way of imprisoning those who think too much of them, but when I talk about being liberated by having less, I'm not simply referring to the things we acquire. Fewer things do mean fewer worries; it's less to maintain and upgrade, to protect and insure. Beyond that, though, is the liberating feeling that comes with no longer having to keep up with the Joneses. We teach our children crucial lessons when we show them that we value thrift, economy, quality, and an environment left for them and their children and future generations to enjoy. The American dream becomes about ingenuity, not about the almighty dollar. That is truly liberating, and it all begins by thinking about a brand new way of defining the word "green."

Use only natural Forest Stewardship Council cedar shingles. (See page 22.)

ABOVE: There are pleasures to living in a house with a small footprint.
OPPOSITE PAGE: Along with the to-die-for stone arch, I love the mix of potted plants and freestyle planting in this hidden courtyard.

Resources

BUILDINGGREEN.COM (http://www.buildinggreen.com/): An independent Brattleboro, Vermont, company that produces GreenSpec, the *Consumer Reports* of building materials.

CO-OP AMERICA (http://www.coopamerica.org/): A Web site that features the National Green Pages, a directory that lists 3,000 retail goods and service providers that are committed to "sustainable, socially just principles."

ENERGY STAR (http://www.energystar.gov/): A Web site run by the EPA and DOE that helps you make energy-efficient choices.

THE FOREST STEWARDSHIP COUNCIL (http://www.fsc.org/): A nonprofit, nongovernmental organization that advances "responsible management of the world's forests."

THE FREECYCLE NETWORK (http://www.freecycle.org/): A free, nonprofit movement with more than 5.5 million members across the globe who donate and obtain items locally.

GOOD TO BE GREEN (http://www.goodtobegreen.com/): A Seattle-based directory for green building products, sustainable building materials, and green building service providers.

GREEN SEAL (http://www.greenseal.org/): A nonprofit organization that rates twenty-one brands of low- and no-VOC paints based on their performance and coverage tests.

HOW TO COMPOST (http://www.howtocompost.org/): A Web site with information about composting.

LIME (http://www.lime.com/): "Healthy living with a twist," a fun, for-profit resource for all things green.

THE PARTNERSHIP FOR ADVANCING TECHNOLOGY IN HOUSING (http://www.pathnet.org/): A voluntary partnership of the homebuilding, product manufacturing, insurance, and financial industries and representatives of federal agencies concerned with housing.

THE RAINFOREST ALLIANCE (http://www.rainforest-alliance.org/): An organization committed to conservation, sustainability, and transformative land use offering examples of model programming as well as numerous resources.

SCIENTIFIC CERTIFICATION SYSTEMS (http://www.scscertified.com/): A for-profit organization that provides third-party environmental, sustainability, and food-quality certification.

THE U.S. GREEN BUILDING COUNCIL (http://www.usgbc.org/): A nonprofit organization comprised of 15,000 member organizations committed to promoting a healthier environment through sustainable building practices. The USBG maintains the LEED Green Building Rating System, which offers universally accepted criteria for green performance.

THE WORLDWATCH INSTITUTE (http://www.worldwatchinstitute.org/): An independent research organization that provides analysis of critical global issues.

Index

A

accessories, 36, 71-72, 92, 116-117

aerator, 21

air purifiers, 127

Alkemi, 50

Amish, 12

appliances, 71

art, 29

B

backsplashes, 54

bamboo, 30, 82, 109, 125

bathrooms

    faucets, 133-134

    furnishings, 134

    furnishings and storage, 143-144

    furniture, salvaging old, 141

    hardwood flooring, 133

    recycled ceramic tiles, 132

    recycled glass tiles, 132

    recycled metal tiles, 133

    refinishing old fixtures, 141

    repurposing, 130

    rubber flooring, 133

    salvaging fixtures, 137

    sinks, 133-134

    tile, replacing, 130-132

    tin ceiling and wall panels, 131

    toilets, 141, 143

    tubs, 137-138

    walls, 133

    walls and floors, 130-132

beadboard, 54, 129, 130

bedrooms

    accessories, 116-117

    air purifiers, 127

    dressers and furniture, 113-115

    floors, 109

    furnishings, 110-112

    lighting, 124

    linens, 122-123

    mattresses, choosing, 116, 120

    open shelving, 116

    personal touches, role of, 104-105

    rugs and carpeting, 109

    vintage beds, 110-113

    walls, 109

    window treatments, 125-126

brick, recycling, 30, 44

C

cabinets, refacing, 57-58

carbon footprint, 21

carbon neutral, 21

Carrera marble, 46

cement countertops, 46

ceramic tiles, recycled, 132

chairs, office, 148

compact fluorescent lightbulb (CFL), 21, 26, 39

composting, 169

concrete, 67

concrete floors, 67

cork, 33

countertops, 46, 50

D

decorating, 42-43, 78

defining, 21

desk set, 148-149

desk surfaces, 148-150

doorknobs, vintage, 32

doormats, 173

doors, 36

dressers and furniture, 113-115

Photo Credits

Lucas Allen: 6, 13, 20, 58, 66, 74 (top left), 90 (right), 96, 102, 117 (middle right), 123, 135, 139, 142, 164 (bottom left), 170, 181

Jim Bastardo: 85 (bottom right)

Ryan Benyi: 5, 12, 15, 27, 31, 50, 56, 64, 65, 80, 85 (top), 90 (top left), 95 (left), 99 (all photos), 112 (bottom right), 117 (bottom right), 120 (left), 125, 158, 159, 176, 179, 185

Justin Bernhaut: 44

John Blais: 121

Adrian Briscoe: 138 (top)

Philip Clayton-Thompson: 182

Jonn Coolidge: 40, 147 (bottom left)

Grey Crawford: 141 (right), 146

Susie Cushner: 55 (top right)

Joseph De Leo: 83, 134 (bottom left)

Dan Duchars/Red Cover Picture Library: 164 (bottom right)

Miki Duisterhof: 45, 161, 164 (top), 166

Hotze Eisma: 147 (bottom right)

Don Freeman: 69, 145, 174

Thayer Allyson Gowdy: 18

Gridley + Graves: 61, 108, 128, 134 (top left), 150, 163

Aimee Herring: 32 (right), 113, 171

Ray Kachatorian: 51, 68 (right)

Keller + Keller: 98 (right), 115 (all photos), 116

Michael Luppino: 26, 55 (bottom right), 75, 133, 160

Andrew McCaul: 111 (bottom)

Ellen McDermott: 8, 10, 14, 25, 34, 37 (top right and bottom right), 38, 41, 47, 59, 62 (both photos), 73, 74 (right), 76, 77, 79, 88-89, 90 (middle left), 95 (right), 101, 106-107, 111 (top), 112 (top), 117 (left), 117 (top right), 118, 120 (right), 130, 134 (middle left), 134 (right), 138 (bottom), 151, 168, 180

Rob Melnychuk: 43

James Merrell: 30, 98 (left)

Alison Miksch: 165

Karyn Millet: 153 (middle right)

Natasha Milne: 85 (bottom left)

Keith Scott Morton: 28, 35, 37 (left), 48-49, 52, 53, 54, 55 (left), 57, 67, 82, 86, 92-94, 105, 112 (bottom left), 114, 119, 122 (left), 124, 126, 131, 140, 144, 147 (top left and top right), 153 (left), 154 (all photos), 155, 156, 177, 178

Laura Moss: 32 (left), 136

David Prince: 97

Olde Good Things: 37 (middle right)

Steven Randazzo: 19, 24, 29, 60, 63, 89 (right), 103, 129, 152, 162

Eric Roth: 16

Kevin Schwasinger: 84, 149

Brad Simmons/Beateworks/Corbis: 141 (left)

William P. Steele: 153 (right top and bottom), 184

Robin Stubbert: 72, 104

Jonny Valiant: 46, 55 (middle right), 68 (left), 70, 74 (bottom left), 81, 91, 110, 122 right, 132, 137, 167, 173

Paul Whicheloe: 90 (bottom left)

Front Cover: (clockwise from upper left) Ellen McDermott, Keith Scott Morton, Lucas Allen, Jonny Valiant, Adrian Briscoe, Steven Randazzo.

Back Cover: (clockwise from upper left) Miki Duisterhof, Ryan Benyi, Jonny Valiant, Ellen McDermott, Ellen McDermott. Center back photo: Jonn Coolidge.

Back Flap: (clockwise from upper left) Ellen McDermott, Natasha Milne, Lucas Allen, Robin Stubbert.